Fundamentals of Buddhism

Fundamentals of Buddhism

Third Edition

NSIC, Tokyo

Nichiren Shoshu International Center
1-33-11 Sendagaya, Shibuya-ku, Tokyo 151

Published 1977. Third Edition 1993
Printed in Japan
97 96 95 94 93   7 6 5 4 3 2 1

ISBN4-88872-034-7 C1015

Contents

Preface

BECAUSE there is a bewildering array of Buddhist teachings—often referred to as the "eighty thousand teachings"—signposts are needed for people to find their way to the essence of Buddhism.

As the title *Fundamentals of Buddhism* indicates, this volume aims to offer such signposts, by means of which a person can gain a comprehensive understanding not only of the Buddhist teachings as a whole but of their ultimate expression—the teachings of Nichiren Daishonin.

There is profound wisdom in the inexhaustible wellspring of Buddhism. To be able to draw on this wisdom is to be able to revitalize human life. This and the attainment of absolute happiness is the purpose of Buddhism; the way to accomplish this purpose is to practice Nichiren Daishonin's Buddhism correctly, always exerting oneself vigorously in both its faith and practice.

Because only a correct practice can lead to absolute happiness, it is important that we practice in accordance with the true spirit of the Daishonin's Buddhism. To this end, a correct understanding of his teachings is indispensable.

Why does Nichiren Daishonin's Buddhism place such great emphasis on practice? Because it is through actual practice that our faith deepens and mere theoretical understanding becomes personal experience engraved in the depths of our lives.

The Buddhism of Nichiren Daishonin has now spread to 115 countries around the world; and as the numbers of people who practice this Buddhism continue to grow, so does the conviction of individual believers that the principles of the Daishonin's Buddhism are universal and that their practical application is endless. We would be most grateful if this volume assists our readers in achieving a fuller, deeper understanding of the Buddhist teachings, and, in this way, richer, happier lives.

Editorial Department
NSIC

Fundamentals of Buddhism

Part One
General Concepts

1. Outline

No clear definition of Buddhism can be readily given. There are many explanations about what Buddhism is, presented from many different angles. Therefore, an attempt to formulate an explanation which is understandable and satisfactory to everyone is a virtual impossibility.

All the teachings of Shakyamuni, the historical founder of Buddhism, were recorded, giving rise to a vast array of sutras or scriptures. Because they contain teachings which are at times contradictory, a large number of schools developed, basing their teachings on one or another of the sutras. As a result, endless controversies arose among the different sects, each asserting the superiority of its own tenets.

Notwithstanding these conflicts, however, all the Buddhist sects commonly acknowledge the account concerning Shakyamuni's motives for renouncing the secular world. It is as follows: In his youth, when he was a prince and called Gautama Siddhārtha, Shakyamuni became aware of and profoundly troubled by the problem of human suffering. He gave up his princely status and pursued the life of a religious mendicant in search of a solution to the four inescapable sufferings which confront all human beings: birth, old age, sickness and death. According to Buddhist tradition, Siddhārtha renounced secular life at the age of nineteen and attained enlightenment at thirty. Modern scholars generally place these ages at twenty-nine and thirty-five, respectively. After eleven years (six years according to the latter view) of ascetic practices and deep meditation, he finally realized the truth which would emancipate human beings from suffering, and he became a Buddha. An understanding of what Buddhism actually is can be gained from knowledge of the motive that prompted him to seek enlightenment. In the final analysis, all of Shakyamuni's teachings were expounded for the sole purpose of solving the universal sufferings of birth, old age, sickness and death, as well as to seek a way to transcend them.

However, this does not mean that Buddhism works to free its believers from the phenomena of aging, sickness and death. Shakyamuni Buddha himself grew old and passed away. He was in no way entirely free of sickness, as is indicated by the statement in the Lotus Sutra, "[The Thus Come One is well and happy,] with few ills and few worries." Then what does it mean to say that Shakyamuni overcame the four sufferings? The answer to this question will clarify the truth to which the Buddha was enlightened, comprising the essence of the Buddha's teachings.

Buddhism has its origin in the desire to solve the most fundamental problem of human suffering. The teachings of Buddhism effectively deal with the question of a human being's very existence and pursue the surest way toward establishing a secure basis for living. There has been a tendency to regard Buddhism as a religion which is nihilistic, negating the value of human life. On the other hand, there are a number of people who think that Buddhism is a means by which to satisfy their material desires. It is true that, among the Buddhist teachings, some speak out against attachment to mundane pursuits and urge people to seek the eternal truth beyond the impermanence of all phenomena, while other teachings assure one of the fulfillment of secular and material desires. However, it is a grave error to think that such teachings constitute the core of Buddhism. The reason for such conflicting views is found in the process by which Shakyamuni's teachings were recorded and transmitted, during which time the essence which integrates all of these partial truths of the Buddha's enlightenment was lost sight of. The purpose and significance of Buddhism lies in overcoming the four basic sufferings of birth, old age, sickness and death, as well as in enabling each individual to establish his own identity.

As stated earlier, the solution to these four sufferings does not mean the denial of the impermanence of life. It is an awakening to the reality of the eternal and essential life which underlies and governs the constant universal cycle of birth, aging, sickness and death. As long as one clings only to the affairs of one's daily existence in this world, one cannot grasp that reality. For this reason, the Buddha taught people to transcend their daily lives, which are uncertain and fleeting, in order to overcome these sufferings. However, to realize the essential life which continues eternally, transcending both birth and death, means to establish the solid foundation of human existence within the harsh realities of this world. One's awakening to the reality of this truth must be reflected in one's daily living. In other words, it manifests itself in such phenomena as the fulfillment of material desires and physical well-being. In this sense, a promise of worldly happiness is also a part of the Buddhist teachings.

In this chapter, based on what has been said above, the Buddhist view of happiness and the human being will be explained, and Buddhist concepts as they apply to philosophy, science and human affairs will be clarified.

2. What Is Buddhism?

BUDDHISM is the name given to the teachings of the Buddha. In other words, Buddhism refers to all the sutras which Shakyamuni Buddha expounded. Unlike other religious philosophies or systems of religious thought, Buddhism makes no clear distinction between divinity and humanity. Its teachings enable people to attain enlightenment, to become Buddhas themselves. But specifically, the Lotus Sutra alone makes Buddhahood accessible to all people. This point will be made clear later in this volume. The Buddha can in no way be defined as a transcendental or supreme being. "Buddha" means the Enlightened One; a Buddha is a person who perceives within his own life the essence, or reality of life. This ultimate reality supports and nourishes humanity and all other living beings. Those who have perceived this ultimate reality inherent in their own lives truly know themselves; they are Buddhas.

Socrates' words, "Know thyself," have posed a problem which philosophy, down through history, has attempted to answer. Buddhism, expounded about one hundred years before the age of Socrates, provided a concrete answer, but it was long obscured by the esoteric tendencies among early Buddhist scholars. The Buddhist philosophy is actually the revelation of a very practical way to bring out the true self, as opposed to the phenomenal self, as one moves toward perfection. It is not metaphysical speculation. Buddhism is basically a practical system of teachings providing a means to realize the ideal state of Buddhahood, which is self-perfection.

Buddhists perceive the ultimate reality of life equally within all human beings, and accordingly respect the dignity of all people. As one begins to recognize this, one understands that one must awaken others to the dignity of their own lives. One's belief urges one to teach and help others awaken to the ultimate reality existing within so that they can create truly happy lives. In that way one is helping others attain Buddhahood. Those who truly strive for the sake of others are called "bodhisattvas." The power which infuses them with the desire to help others is the impartial and infinite compassion of the Buddha called *jihi*.

The two goals of Buddhism, then, are the attainment of Buddhahood and the fulfillment of the requirements of the bodhisattva. Interestingly, they are restated in Immanuel Kant's idea that self-perfection and other people's happiness are at once the purposes and obligations of human beings, unconsciously echoing principles expounded at least 2,300 years before Kant's time. This shows that a universal teaching can and will reappear in entirely different cultural mediums.

3. Shakyamuni's Life and Mission

THERE can be, and in fact are, more than one Buddha. The first Buddha in recorded history is known by the name Shakyamuni. He realized the ultimate reality of life, and his teachings have collectively come to be called Buddhism. Approximately three thousand years ago, he was born the son of King Shuddhodana, who reigned over the kingdom of the Shākyas, one of the minor kingdoms in India at that time. *Shakya* of Shakyamuni derives from the name of the tribe to which he belonged, and *muni* means a sage or one who is awakened. At birth he was named Gautama Siddhārtha by his parents, Gautama being his family name and Siddhārtha, which meant "goal achieved," his given name. He was honored with the name Shakyamuni, the sage of the Shākyas, only after he attained enlightenment.

Though still very young, Siddhārtha was so unusually clever that he quickly saw that he and all others were equally confronted with four inescapable problems in life—birth (into this trouble-ridden world), old age, sickness and death. Although surrounded by luxury, he was driven by an irresistible desire to do something about these sufferings, so he renounced his royal heritage, his luxurious surroundings and even his family. Longing to attain enlightenment, he began to follow a life of self-denial in the manner of the ascetics of his day. After pursuing the ascetic life for a considerable time, he found it to be useless. He returned to a more moderate way of living and engaged in deep meditation until finally he attained his goal. In order to transmit to all people the enlightenment which he had attained, he taught for fifty years, leaving behind him many teachings.

Before he could reveal the depths of his enlightenment, Shakyamuni had to prepare his disciples thoroughly. The truth of life was much too difficult for the ordinary person to comprehend merely through intellect. People had immersed themselves in immediate pleasures, thinking these pleasures to be the happiness that they were seeking. Therefore it was imperative for Shakyamuni to bring them face to face with the harsh realities of life in this world. He taught how vain it was to live a life filled with pain, only to die and to repeat the same cycle again and again throughout time. The logical conclusion of these first teachings, known as Hinayana Buddhism, was that the only way to escape from suffering was to eliminate desire. This meant to annihilate even one's body because it was the seat of all desires. People were taught to long for the state of nothingness. These teachings were a primitive introduction to the more profound concept of non-substantiality (kū).

As his disciples began to understand his teaching in

greater depth, Shakyamuni discouraged them from seeking the "void." He taught them that there was another world quite apart from this trouble-ridden and transitory world. One would be reborn, as he put it, in an eternal and happy world in the eastern or the western part of the universe even without extinguishing desires. His followers came to long for such a heavenly paradise after their death. These teachings comprised part of the provisional doctrines of Mahayana Buddhism.

A radical change took place when Shakyamuni brought forth what was later known as the Lotus Sutra. He encouraged his disciples to turn inward toward their own "life," instead of outward toward some external world. He taught that if they realized the ultimate reality within their own lives, even the world they inhabited would become an eternally peaceful land.

Yet, even then Shakyamuni remained silent about what the ultimate reality of life actually was. It was not until another Buddha, Nichiren Daishonin, appeared that the ultimate reality was thoroughly and completely clarified.

4. Nichiren Daishonin's Buddhism

NICHIREN Daishonin was born on February 16, 1222, in the village of Kominato in Awa Province in present-day Chiba Prefecture. In contrast to Shakyamuni, born the son of a king, Nichiren Daishonin's parents made their living by fishing. In Japan in this period fishermen and hunters were despised because their livelihood involved the taking of life. The circumstances of his birth are highly significant, for they indicate the Buddhist principle of the ultimate equality of all people, regardless of social status or other superficial standards.

He was given the childhood name Zennichi-maro and lived in the fishing village until 1233, when, at the age of twelve,* he left home to study both Buddhist and secular teachings at a nearby temple called Seichō-ji.

In the course of his studies, he perceived various contradictions among the Buddhist teachings; he also determined to find an answer to the problem of the transience of human life, about which he was deeply concerned. Around this time, he prayed before a statue of Bodhisattva Kokūzō (Space Repository) enshrined at Seichō-ji to become the wisest man in Japan. Because of these prayers he obtained a "jewel of wisdom" which later enabled him to grasp the essence of all the sutras. After much study and contemplation, he realized the nature of the ultimate reality of life and the universe. Taking this awakening as his starting point, he resolved to pursue his studies to enable him to present his ideas systematically.

In 1237 he became a Buddhist priest and took the name Zeshō-bō Renchō. In 1242, after spending a few years in Kamakura—then the governmental center of Japan—to further his Buddhist studies, he returned to Seichō-ji. Feeling an urgent need to continue his studies, he left the same year for Kyoto and Nara, the two

*According to the traditional Japanese system of reckoning age, a baby is one year old at the time of birth, and a year is added to its age with each ensuing New Year's Day. Thus when the Daishonin entered the temple, he was actually only eleven years old.

centers of traditional Buddhism in Japan. There he remained until 1253, by which time he felt that he had discovered what he had long sought: irrefutable documentary proof that the doctrines of the various sects are not in fact based on the teachings of the founder of Buddhism and that the true teachings of Buddhism are to be found in the Lotus Sutra only.

Having returned to Seichō-ji, convinced that the time had come to reveal his discoveries to others, the Daishonin, early on the morning of April 28, 1253, there chanted Nam-myoho-renge-kyo for the first time—thus showing the direct path to enlightenment for all humanity, for all generations to come. At this point, he declared that none of the pre-Lotus Sutra teachings revealed the Buddha's enlightenment and that all Buddhist sects based on such teachings were misguided. He also took on the name Nichiren.

Nichi of Nichiren signifies the sun or the light cast by the wisdom of Nichiren Daishonin across the entire world to eliminate the darkness that afflicts humankind. *Ren* means lotus; it indicates that Nichiren Daishonin appeared within the corrupt and strife-ridden world in order to cause the pure and beautiful flowers of wisdom and culture to blossom forth from within the troubled hearts of all people. *Ren* also symbolizes the law of cause and effect at work within the depths of life. And it is a part of the title of the Lotus Sutra, *Myoho-renge-kyo*.

Having thus established and begun to propagate the true teachings of Buddhism, the Daishonin encountered persecution of the severest kind, both from other Buddhist sects popular at the time and from government authorities who were their patrons and who relied on them for prayers for the cessation of current ongoing disasters.

Nichiren Daishonin spent over two decades teaching people about his Buddhism and remonstrating with the government—so that its leaders might bring peace to the nation by accepting the true teachings of Buddhism. During this period he survived two exiles, an attempted execution, ambush, and numerous attempts to discredit him. Finally, on May 12, 1274, Nichiren Daishonin left Kamakura for the remote mountain site of Minobu where he was to carry out the final stage of his activities.

There, in 1279, Nichiren Daishonin inscribed the Dai-Gohonzon—the object of worship for all humankind. By this time, there were disciples and followers willing to risk their lives to embrace and spread Nammyoho-renge-kyo. He was confident, then, that these strong believers would protect his teaching for all posterity.

Three years later, on the morning of October 13, 1282, at the home of a believer in a part of present-day Tokyo, Nichiren Daishonin passed away peacefully.

We might define his role in the stream of Buddhist thought and history as follows: Nichiren Daishonin was the Buddha awakened to the ultimate truth of life since the infinite past; this was an incalculably long period before Shakyamuni Buddha attained his enlightenment at a time in the distant past called *gohyaku-jintengō*. The Daishonin defined this truth as Nam-myoho-renge-kyo and embodied it in the form of the Gohonzon.

In the Lotus Sutra, it is predicted that when the Latter Day of the Law arrives, the Bodhisattvas of the Earth will appear to bring salvation to all humankind. The leader of these bodhisattvas, Jōgyō, is Nichiren Daishonin.

Because he attained enlightenment by himself—through his own understanding—and because he revealed the fundamental truth of life, Nichiren Daishonin is called the original Buddha. And because he manifested the benevolence proper to a bodhisattva by propagating the ultimate teaching of Buddhism in society, leading the people toward enlightenment, he is identified as Bodhisattva Jōgyō.

5. Enlightenment

ENLIGHTENMENT as taught in Buddhism means to come to a full and positive awareness of the Buddhahood present in all human beings. Scriptures refer to the Buddha's enlightenment by the Sanskrit term *anuttara-samyak-sambodhi,* which means "perfect and unsurpassed wisdom." The Lotus Sutra states that people can attain this enlightenment by believing in the teachings of the sutra, which reveal that inherent Buddhahood. Further developing this doctrine, Nichiren Daishonin taught that to believe beyond any doubt that Nam-myoho-renge-kyo, the essence of the Lotus Sutra, exists within one's life is in itself enlightenment and the manifestation of Buddhahood.

The Lotus Sutra states that belief is a means to attain enlightenment, but in Nichiren Daishonin's Buddhism, belief is in itself enlightenment. The reason for the difference is that Shakyamuni's teachings led people toward the understanding of the Mystic Law, but they did not clearly reveal it; Nichiren Daishonin, however, embodied the Mystic Law or ultimate reality of the universe, Nam-myoho-renge-kyo, in the Gohonzon. Therefore, the Gohonzon is itself the entity of this Law. By chanting daimoku or the invocation of Nam-myoho-renge-kyo with strong faith in the Gohonzon, one can attain Buddhahood. This is enlightenment. Nichikan Shonin, the twenty-sixth high priest of Taiseki-ji, said, "Strong faith in the Lotus Sutra [the Gohonzon] is in itself Buddhahood."

People tend to think that upon attaining enlightenment they will suddenly understand all the events in their past, present and future. However, to "penetrate the three existences of life," according to the Gosho, the writings of Nichiren Daishonin, actually means to comprehend the ultimate reality of life which is unchangeable throughout all time. If people understand the true entity of their lives, they can live wisely and deal with any situation effectively. Such enlightenment manifests itself as inexhaustible wisdom which illuminates every aspect of one's own existence and the society in which one lives.

It has been said that Jōsei Toda, the second president of the Soka Gakkai, "attained enlightenment" in prison, but that does not mean he attained Buddhahood at that specific time. Since he had been a believer in the Gohonzon for years before his imprisonment, he was certainly already in the process of bringing forth the state of Buddhahood. Rather, what he experienced in prison was a great awakening or insight. One thing he achieved in prison was a deep understanding of what the entity of the Buddha means to contemporary people. Another was a sense of the purpose for which he came into the world and a firmer grasp of the reason why he had to suffer imprisonment; he recognized that both his life and the sufferings he had to endure were for the sake of his mission to propagate Nichiren Daishonin's Buddhism throughout the world.

6. Faith and Reason

ONE of the underlying assumptions of Buddhist thinking is that every person can and must strive to be united with the truth (the Law of life and the universe), not through an intermediary, such as Jesus Christ of Christian belief, but directly, by becoming a Buddha, one who is in complete harmony with the Law of life.

Wisdom, with which one grasps the Law of life, comes forth from the depths of one's own life and is crucial in the attainment of Buddhahood. A person who makes great efforts to grasp the Law is called a bodhisattva. *Bodhi* of bodhisattva means wisdom and *sattva* means living beings. Bodhisattva means one who aspires to attain wisdom. On fully attaining the truth, one is called a Buddha. The wisdom of the Buddha is called in Sanskrit *anuttara-samyak-sambodhi,* which means the supreme, perfect and universal wisdom to perceive the Law of the universe.

FAITH AND REASON   17

Buddhism thus expounds the virtue of wisdom and teaches how one can gain that wisdom. But Hinayana doctrines expound only the knowledge of analysis and logic of the phenomenal world. *Shrāvaka* (voice-hearers) and *pratyekabuddha* (cause-awakened ones) possess this level of wisdom. Reason has much in common with Hinayana Buddhist wisdom. However, in the *Hōben* (second) chapter of the Lotus Sutra Shakyamuni declared that the Buddha wisdom is beyond the reach of analysis. He then revealed that only through faith can one fully attain the Buddha wisdom. With faith one can open the inner palace of life, the palace of Buddhahood. Buddhahood is cultivated by belief, and all one needs to do to attain Buddhahood is to establish unyielding faith in the Gohonzon.

Nichiren Daishonin identified the supreme wisdom of Buddhahood as Nam-myoho-renge-kyo, but this wisdom is difficult to communicate to other people. Therefore, it is necessary to clarify one's innate wisdom by employing the knowledge which people use in their activities in society today. One's faith, or one's ultimate intuitive wisdom, will lead one to Buddhahood, but in order to lead others to the Law of life, one must often utilize analytic reasoning. Shakyamuni and Nichiren Daishonin used reason to expound the sutras and the Gosho, respectively, and wisdom to lead humankind to the Law of life.

7. Meaning of Faith

GENERALLY speaking, "believing" means the acceptance of a truth or premise which is beyond pure rationale. But belief does not end with mere acceptance; rather, it leads one to consider what actions one should take on the basis of this truth or premise.

Many people are brought up to think that "believing" is equal to blind obedience. It is often the case that followers of a given religion or cult regard their founder as perfect, free from mistakes, and as a result they obey him and his dictates, or the "rules" of the group, without question. Blind obedience is dangerous because it means subordinating one's own will to that of another. Moreover, belief in a transcendental being can cause one to ignore or try to escape the world one lives in. As long as the object to be worshiped is a transcendental existence, followers may attach greater importance to obedience than to understanding. They tend to become more concerned with a world other than the present one. Such belief simply means giving up one's will and yielding oneself completely to the will of a prophet or a transcendental, and possibly nonexistent, being. It is nothing but blind faith.

Buddhism rejects faith in an individual being. The object of faith should be the universal Law immanent in both human life and the universe. Shakyamuni and Nichiren Daishonin both admonished people to believe in the Law and not in any particular person. This admonition shows how important the object of faith is.

The Chinese character for faith has two meanings.

One is not to deceive, that is, to be truthful, and the other is not to doubt. Buddhism does not, however, force one to blindly discard all doubts. Descartes started by doubting everything, and arrived at the conclusion: "I think, therefore I am." So saying, he had in mind the image of his own thinking self—reason—as the only ultimate truth he could not doubt. Miao-lo of China is quoted in one of Nichiren Daishonin's writings as saying: "To 'believe in the perfect teaching' means to awaken faith through doctrine and make faith the basis of practice."* Buddhist faith opposes irrationality, and accords perfectly with reason in every area that reason can penetrate, as well as requiring the acceptance of a suprarational truth.

In his *Hokke mongu* (Words and Phrases of the Lotus Sutra), the Great Teacher T'ien-t'ai states, "Having no doubt is called belief." "Belief without doubt" in this passage means ultimate belief which one attains after resolving all doubts. This passage may seem to demand blind faith. Buddhism does indeed deny the value of doubt for the sake of doubt, but it never denies the value of doubt that arises from the desire to arrive at the truth. One should never be swayed by doubt to the extent that one neglects the pursuit of the truth. Instead, view doubt as a tool with which to discover the truth. One should use doubt rather than let it overtake one. "Belief without doubt" is the ultimate belief which one can attain after one has completely resolved all one's doubts.

Shakyamuni revealed his enlightenment in the Lotus

The Major Writings of Nichiren Daishonin (hereafter cited as *Major Writings*), vol. 1, p. 214.

Sutra. He also stated that the Lotus Sutra was his only true teaching and enjoined his disciples to believe in this teaching alone. What is the truth revealed in the Lotus Sutra? It is that the Buddha nature and the Buddha wisdom are inherent in the depths of all people's lives, and that by manifesting this Buddha nature and Buddha wisdom all people can become Buddhas without discarding their present identity. How can one manifest one's inherent Buddha nature and Buddha wisdom? The means was taught by Nichiren Daishonin, who revealed that the Buddha nature and Buddha wisdom are Nam-myoho-renge-kyo. He embodied Nam-myoho-renge-kyo in the concrete form of the Gohonzon and taught that the Buddha nature and wisdom may be manifested by chanting daimoku with the conviction that one's life is also the entity of Nam-myoho-renge-kyo. Thus, he showed the way for all people to attain Buddhahood.

8. Good Fortune and Benefit

THE purpose of Buddhism is to enable all people to attain the same state as the Buddha, to attain supreme wisdom, thereby awakening them to the Law of individual and universal life to which the Buddha is enlightened. This is what is meant by the term Buddhahood, the ultimate benefit of faith. To attain Buddhahood, however, is quite beyond the understanding of ordinary people, and thus the power of Buddhism must be proven in everyday life so that all people can understand its greatness. In Nichiren Daishonin's Buddhism, "benefit" and "punishment"—gain and loss or positive values and negative values—are the expedient means by which people are led to the ultimate goal of enlightenment.

The reformation of life brought about by the practice of Buddhism always manifests itself in daily life. What are called benefits are the visible results of life's inner changes. Even believers do not gain great benefits unless they achieve human revolution and individual growth. Buddhism does not directly bring about the visible changes or benefits; rather, it induces inner reformation, the first and most fundamental of all reformations. Buddhism has the power to bring about such inner revolution, but a noticeable change in one's everyday life can only result from the power gained through such self-reformation.

These fundamental changes are called inconspicuous benefits and they are difficult to perceive. Nichiren Daishonin defines "benefit" as the purification of one's six senses—sight, hearing, smell, taste, touch and consciousness—saying in effect that benefit lies in the purification of all the mental and physical functions of life. In the "Ongi kuden" (Record of the Orally Transmitted Teachings) Nichiren Daishonin referred to two essentials, "good fortune" and "wisdom," as the major benefits of Buddhist practice. The power of self-reformation is essentially the power of wisdom. It is important to remember that one's life force and life space are not limited to the physical body but extend outward to include one's social and natural environment. A change in one's life automatically influences one's environment, and this environmental change is the meaning of good fortune. The Chinese character for good fortune signifies the fullness of the gods, or in Buddhism, the powers inherent in the environment.

Benefits are divided into two categories: wisdom, which indicates the reformation of human life, and good fortune, which means the reformation of one's environment. Reformations in the environment are usually caused by changes in human life itself.

There are cases, however, where the environment changes irrespective of one's inner changes, but these are exceptional. These positive changes in the environment are included in the concept of conspicuous benefits. This kind of benefit appears when a believer's life is in danger, when the correctness of the teachings of true Buddhism must be demonstrated, and when proof of the Gohonzon must be shown to new believers. An example of the first instance was when Nichiren Daishonin narrowly escaped execution at Tatsunokuchi; an example of the second, the victory of the power of his teachings, occurred when the Daishonin was successful in his prayers for rain.

9. Attainment of Buddhahood

UNIQUE to Nichiren Daishonin's Buddhism is the possibility of attaining Buddhahood in this lifetime. This principle is indicated specifically in the Lotus Sutra.

Among the sutras expounded before the Lotus Sutra,

Hinayana teachings emphasize the state of arhat, the highest stage of enlightenment which voice-hearers aim to achieve through their Buddhist practice. The Mahayana sutras in general describe the practices leading to enlightenment as extending over a period of countless kalpas. The early Mahayana teachings assert that bodhisattva practices are impossible to carry out in this impure world, and set forth the practice by which to attain rebirth in an ideal world such as the Pure Land of Perfect Bliss in the west. The later Mahayana sutras, however, describe practices that people can carry out within the realities of this present world, though the process is still a very long one. They teach that, by following six kinds of practices, bodhisattvas can gradually elevate their state of life over a period of many kalpas and become that much closer to enlightenment. This process is divided into fifty-two stages: ten stages of faith, ten stages of security, ten stages of practice, ten stages of devotion, ten stages of development, the stage of near-perfect enlightenment and the stage of perfect enlightenment. The six practices are called the six *pāramitās* and are required of bodhisattvas in order to attain Buddhahood. It takes a great many kalpas for a bodhisattva to complete each of these fifty-two stages.

The question, then, is how long one must carry out the six *pāramitās*. In the Mahayana scriptures, there is a story of Shāriputra, who was known as the foremost in wisdom among Shakyamuni's disciples. According to this story, Shāriputra engaged in the offering of alms, one of the six *pāramitās,* in the distant past, and he had to continue this practice for one hundred kalpas. A kalpa is an unimaginably large unit of time, which equals approximately sixteen million years. (There are differing views as to the length of a kalpa.) Therefore, one hundred kalpas is about 1.6 billion years. Shāriputra could not continue his practice of almsgiving for all of these kalpas. When he had practiced for sixty kalpas, a Brahman begged Shāriputra to give him one of his eyes. Shāriputra complied, but the Brahman threw the eye down on the ground and trampled on it. Seeing this, Shāriputra harbored doubts about the significance of almsgiving and abandoned his practice. This story has many lessons concerning one's Buddhist practice. However, it is astounding to learn how long it takes to complete the six *pāramitās.* If these six practices each require one hundred kalpas, then it takes 9.6 billion years to complete them all.

In contrast, the *Muryōgi* Sutra (Sutra of Infinite Meaning), which serves as the prologue to the Lotus Sutra, states, "Although they have not yet been able to practice the six *pāramitās,* the six *pāramitās* will of themselves appear before them." The Lotus Sutra then proceeds to reveal the one ultimate Law which contains all the benefits of the six *pāramitās.* Only through single-minded faith in and lifelong practice of this Law can all people obtain the same benefits as those of the six *pāramitās* and attain Buddhahood within this lifetime. The one Law indicated in the Lotus Sutra is none other than Nam-myoho-renge-kyo, which Nichiren Daishonin realized and manifested.

10. Six *Pāramitās*

THE Sanskrit word *pāramitā* signifies "having reached the opposite shore." In Buddhism, the world of a deluded common mortal is compared to "this shore," while that of a Buddha, the enlightened one, is compared to "the other shore." Bodhisattva practices are likened to the process of crossing from the shore of delusion to the shore of enlightenment. The six *pāramitās,* then, are those practices which bodhisattvas must carry out in order to attain Buddhahood.

The first of the six *pāramitās* is the offering of alms. This means making offerings, both material and spiritual, for the salvation of suffering people. In the offering of alms, one must give according to what one's recipient seeks. Therefore, almsgiving does not simply indicate sharing one's property with other people but includes preaching the Law to them, removing their fears and giving them relief. The second *pāramitā* is the observance of precepts. This means faithfully observing all the precepts that are laid down. Keeping the precepts may also be taken to signify practicing the correct rules of behavior and the right ways of living so that one does not have to undergo suffering. The precepts include all the rules of discipline pertaining to physical, verbal and spiritual acts or states. The third *pāramitā* is forbearance. This implies bearing up patiently under all opposition and hardships that arise to obstruct one's practice. The fourth is assiduousness. This means constantly exerting oneself with a pure mind to advance along the correct path. The fifth is meditation. This indicates focusing one's mind and contemplating the truth with a tranquil heart. The last of the six *pāramitās* is the obtaining of wisdom. This refers to acquiring sufficient wisdom to perceive the true nature of all things and correctly recognize the truth.

The purpose of the six *pāramitās* as set forth in the Mahayana teachings other than the Lotus Sutra is to reach the shore of enlightenment through the pursuit of these practices. However, the Lotus Sutra reveals that, by believing in and embracing the one single Law, the Mystic Law, one will be able to obtain all the benefits of these six kinds of practices and attain enlightenment quickly. In Nichiren Daishonin's Buddhism as well, the six *pāramitās* do not have to be practiced to realize enlightenment. The Daishonin teaches that those who practice the Mystic Law with correct faith can naturally become endowed with the benefits of the six *pāramitās*. Therefore, in terms of the Daishonin's teaching, the six *pāramitās* are interpreted to signify moral qualities which a human being should possess. The Buddha is a supreme being completely endowed with all these requirements.

"This shore" represents the six paths—Hell, Hunger, Animality, Anger, Humanity and Heaven—along which a deluded common mortal moves, constantly shuttling from one to another. "The other shore" of enlightenment is likened to the world of Buddhahood, and those who are crossing the sea between "this shore" and "the other shore" by pursuing the practice of the six *pāramitās* are the people who are in the realm of Bodhisattva. In contrast, those of the two vehicles (voice-hearers and cause-awakened ones) who seek only their own happiness can be defined as those who are drifting toward a different direction from "the other shore," although they have succeeded in leaving "this shore" of delusion and embarking on a voyage toward enlightenment.

11. Meaning of Happiness

WHEN one's needs or wishes are fulfilled, one feels happy, but mere fulfillment of desires cannot sustain this feeling of happiness. Even though a person is not fully satisfied with his present life, he may feel that he is happier than he used to be. Still, no one is continually happy. No matter how much better things are, there are bound to be unpleasant moments.

Such happiness is essentially relative. Deeper and more lasting happiness depends neither on the object of desire or need, nor on one's past, nor on the life of one's neighbor, nor on any other external factor. The major ingredient of such happiness is within one's own life. Happiness is directly related to the degree one can draw on one's own life force and the hope one has for the future. Conversely, if one does not have these qualities, one compares one's present with the past or with one's surroundings. Happiness-by-comparison is, in the very real sense of the term, "relative happiness."

To understand the difference that one's own life force can make, imagine two mountain climbers. Climbing a precipitous peak would inflict unbearable pain on an ordinary person, yet it can give unforgettable pleasure to a cragsman. The higher, steeper and more difficult the cliff, the greater the joy and satisfaction of challenging and conquering it. Difficulties in life are like the precipitous mountain. If one finds happiness only in comfort, one will be avoiding much that is worthwhile in life. Such an attitude is essentially negative and escapist. When we come right down to it, comfort is a period of rest and is accompanied by neither great pain nor deep joy.

All human activities aim at happiness. Buddhism, like other religions, teaches people how to live to attain a happy life. However, most religions encourage their believers to pray that some mystic, transcendental force will remove their problems in life. Then, too, whether people are religious or not, they often try to avoid hardships and problems. Buddhism shows the way to cultivate youthful vitality and deep wisdom, teaching that human beings must become inspired to challenge, not to avoid, whatever difficulties they face and to turn them into happiness through the development of their own life force. It is a creative attitude of challenge and courage to try and surmount suffering rather than turn away from it, and it is this attitude that leads to absolute happiness.

12. Buddhist Concept of Law

SHAKYAMUNI, death close at hand, left his disciples instructions saying that, rather than relying on a particular person as their master, they should rely on the Law as their teacher. The word "law," as used in Buddhism, has a very broad meaning. It is the English equivalent for the Sanskrit word *dharma,* which means the teachings of the Buddha as well as the truth underlying all phenomena. "Law" as used in everyday life means rules laid down to protect the individual and support the institutions of a group or nation. The European idea of natural law, however, is based on the assumption of a greater law conceived by God and manifested in nature and human society.

The Judeo-Christian religions, which postulate a Creator of the universe, hold that the laws governing natural phenomena were also made by God. These religions also generally hold that the laws of human society were established by human beings acting on behalf of God.

The law as taught in Buddhism was not laid down by any specified "being." The Buddhist law has inherently existed as the core of the universe. It is the cause and supporter of all that exists. Here one can see why the Buddhist idea of the law also means the teachings expounded by the Buddha; the Buddha neither created nor laid down the law, but clarified the law originally governing the universe. Therefore, the teachings expounded by the Buddha can be defined as the "Law." The law in this sense is more like the idea of truth within the realm of the natural sciences rather than so-called laws of jurisprudence. To view the Buddhist "Law" in this way enables us to understand that norms or laws in daily life, in order to work harmoniously, must accord with the truths contained in the essential nature of a human being and all phenomena. Laws in the realms of politics, jurisprudence and social science should not be arbitrarily laid down by any special person or authority but should be established on the basis of insight that penetrates the truth underlying the existence of human life.

There exist many truths, extending from the specific or phenomenal to the universal and essential. At the deepest level of life, the fundamental truth which supports all universal phenomena and laws is the Mystic Law as indicated in the Lotus Sutra, and a Buddha is a person who is enlightened to it.

13. Law of Causality

BUDDHISM teaches that human happiness is based on the law of cause and effect. Different from the concept of causality in the natural or social sciences, the Buddhist principle of cause and effect concerns one's inner life first and foremost.

Suppose a student studies hard for an examination and passes it with high marks. Diligent study is the cause, and passing is the effect. But there is always some medium which connects the cause to the effect, and in this case the medium is the act of taking the examination. A medium as such functions in two ways: It produces an effect and contributes to forming a new cause. The same amount of effort, however, does not necessarily lead to the same results. Some students naturally have good memories, while others tend to forget things quickly. The important question is what produces such differences between individuals. Buddhism attributes the cause to one's way of life in previous existences. One's individuality and natural abilities are the effects of causes established in previous lifetimes.

In this regard, Buddhism is very different from the doctrine of some Western religions which hold that a transcendental being predetermines the course of one's life in this world. Buddhism asserts that each individual is responsible for his own destiny and at the same time has the prerogative to change it for the better and develop his character in the future. This means that a person with a weak memory does not have to resign himself to his fate. If he realizes his weak point, he may start preparations for a test earlier than others so that he can memorize the study materials effectively and completely. Thus, he will be able to overcome his disadvantage. Instead of depending on his weak memory, he can compensate for it by improving his understanding. By being aware of one's own strengths, weaknesses and inclinations, it is possible to develop the strong points and improve the weak ones. This is the correct way to surmount the restraints of destiny. Even so, one must have enough power to enjoy freedom by making the law of cause and effect work to one's advantage.

Nichiren Daishonin elucidated the way to increase one's life force and wisdom so as to be able to attain freedom far beyond what one can attain with conscious effort alone. Since destiny is the product, or effect, of one's past efforts as determined by the law of causality, one cannot avoid its effects. Nonetheless, one does not have to be resigned. If one stands firmly on the riverbed of life, the Mystic Law that is the entity of life, not even the torrents of karma, or destiny, can carry one away. By establishing an unshakable foundation, one gains the liberty to act on one's own will.

14. Fatalism and Freedom

SOME people hold that human affairs are completely predetermined, a way of thinking regarded as fatalistic. For similar reasons the Buddhist view of causation is sometimes criticized as being fatalistic. If one's life in this world is predestined as the result of causes in the past, and if one's future is determined by one's present karma-bound life, where can one find freedom and what meaning can one seek in life?

A typical example of fatalism can be found in some of the pre-Lotus Sutra teachings. Those teachings state that the only salvation is found in life after death. For example, it was said that if a person believed and relied on the grace of such a Buddha as Amida, he would gain freedom from the fetters of this world and be reborn in the Pure Land of Perfect Bliss. But there is no rational support for such a belief. Freedom is found, not by trying to escape causation, but by turning it to our advantage.

No one can escape the law of causation, but human beings can learn how it works and utilize it. Throughout history, individuals have discovered and put into application various laws of nature, such as the law of gravity and the theory of relativity. Gravity can be thought of as a force holding people to the earth, but it can also be seen as the force which makes possible the freedom to move on land, across the seas and in the air.

Shakyamuni states, "If you want to understand the causes that existed in the past, look at the results as they are manifested in the present. And if you want to understand what results will be manifested in the future, look at the causes that exist in the present." There exists, then, the absolute possibility of changing one's future through one's present efforts. But what can be done about the causes one has already formed in the past? One's personality, character and destiny are all results of what one was and what one did in the past. In the Lotus Sutra Shakyamuni directed people to a source of power which can sever the chains of karmic forces, but he did not specifically identify it. It was Nichiren Daishonin who explained the entity of life, as opposed to life's phenomena, and how it remains for all eternity free from karmic influences. This entity or Law of life, which he called Nam-myoho-renge-kyo, is the cause which enables one to overcome all karmic inertia and allows new effects to be brought out of the life of every human being. The struggle to overcome the inertia of evil causes created since ages past is naturally a difficult one and requires lifelong effort. Yet the fact that this struggle is certain to result in victory dispels one's feeling of fatalism and brings hope for a bright future.

The word *renge* (literally, the lotus flower) of Nam-myoho-renge-kyo symbolizes the principle that cause and effect exist simultaneously in a single moment of life. Therefore, it means that one's will in the present will determine one's future, or the effect for which one is striving. Is one's determination strong enough to change one's destiny? Will power operates in the conscious levels of the human psyche, while karma exists in the unconscious levels, or even deeper. Clearly humankind needs some power which can alter the flow of life itself, and that power is and always has been Nam-myoho-renge-kyo. With the awareness of this powerful key to human beings' inherent inexhaustible life force, people can be confident that they can form causes to emancipate themselves totally from their negative karma. With this key, all that remains is to draw the life energy of Nam-myoho-renge-kyo out of the depths of their own lives. This is possible through the steady, sincere chanting of daimoku to the Gohonzon, the embodiment of Nam-myoho-renge-kyo.

15. God and Buddha

RELIGIONS of the world vary in accordance with the differences among nations and cultures. However, the origin of religion itself can be found in feelings shared by all people. The most primitive form of religion was the worship of a god or gods representing the forces of nature. As long as nature underwent "normal," predictable change, human beings were able to enjoy its creative power and benefits. However, when nature's rhythm grew unpredictable, people had nowhere to turn. Ancient peoples regarded natural calamities as expressions of their god's anger or as the work of a diabolic, destructive god, who opposed their benevolent god. Through continued speculation, some postulated a

chief god reigning over all others and controlling nature's various phenomena. In many cases, the chief god
originally ruled a specific phenomenon. For example, in
the Greek and Norse mythologies the chief god was
originally the god of thunder.

The same is said of Yahweh or Jehovah. Yahweh was
originally the god of thunder and later became the chief
god for the ancient predecessors of the Hebrews. He
was eventually considered to be an absolute and transcendental god by the Jews and finally the only god, his
followers denying the existence of any other god. This
led to the formation of the belief that God's will and
words created the universe and all beings within it.
Whether it was one god or many, the deity or deities
were thought of as having controlling power over nature and humankind. With the establishment of com-
munities some gods became symbols of the power or
supremacy of specified groups, being used to strength-
en the group's authority.

In contrast, a Buddha is a human being, one who has
developed introspective wisdom into the depths of his
life and discovered the eternal truth therein. Whereas
in Christianity a human being can never become God
completely, in Buddhism a human being can become a
Buddha. Buddhahood is an ideal, but one which human
beings can attain. Buddhism is the body of teachings
which the Buddha expounded in order to enable all
people to become Buddhas as well. It teaches that
Buddhahood is the ultimate goal for all human beings;
however, it does not deny or exclude the concept of a
god per se. What characterizes the Buddha is the wisdom which penetrates the ultimate truth of life and the

universe. Buddhism describes gods as beneficial forces
innate in social and natural surroundings which work
to protect human beings, especially those who practice Buddhism correctly. The powers inherent in the
environment are referred to as "good fortune," the
workings of the Buddhist gods which one activates by
bringing forth one's own Buddha wisdom.

16. A Comparison between Christianity and Buddhism

CHRISTIANITY expounds the ideal of love for all humankind, especially for the less fortunate and unhappy.
Christian love has much in common with Buddhist
compassion. Because of his love, Jesus of Nazareth is
comparable to a bodhisattva. As far as its universal love
is concerned, Christianity is much closer to the ideals of
Buddhism than to Judaism.

There are two historical currents of Buddhism—
northern and southern. The first originated in the
northern part of India, then spread via Central Asia to
China, to Korea and finally to Japan, whereas Southern
Buddhism found its way into Ceylon (Sri Lanka),
Burma and Indochina. These two streams of Buddhism
are also known as Mahayana and Hinayana Buddhism.

Very little is known about the western course of Buddhist propagation. However, some historical records
show that King Ashoka of India dispatched Buddhist
messengers to as far away as Greece. Some Western

scholars believe that there is some Buddhist influence within Christianity.

Some modern Christian theologians interpret God not as a human-like being but as a "law," immaterial and universal, which influences phenomena throughout the universe. This view has more in common with Buddhist ideas, and the fact that it developed at all indicates that there may be some deep connection between the two streams of thought.

That possibility still remains to be objectively proven, but the similarity of the teachings of the two religions is important. For instance, the kingdom of God is startlingly similar to the description of the Western Paradise in provisional Mahayana teachings expounded before the Lotus Sutra. Also the Christian teachings and commandments seem equally to describe the way a Western bodhisattva should live.

17. The Relationship between Philosophy and Religion

FRANCIS M. Cornford, a professor at Cambridge, as well as other Western historians of philosophy, has demonstrated how philosophy originated from religion in ancient Greece. Behind the ideas of Socrates, Plato and Pythagoras were the doctrines of their religion. In a similar way, Western philosophy began to develop out of Christian theology toward the close of the Middle Ages.

The myths, rituals and teachings passed down from ancient times represent the intuition or insight of the people. Those who believed there was truth in them attempted to put them into practice. This is the origin of religion. In contrast, philosophy developed through efforts to shed new light on those truths, systematize them, and discover new truths through its own methodology. Philosophers very early tried to find a universal, all-inclusive truth immanent in all phenomena, and then their concepts gradually grew more complex with a new concern for the surroundings. Perhaps influenced by the development of natural science, as well as stimulating it, some philosophers concentrated on trying to grasp partial truths of the phenomenal world. In a sense, science is at once the child of philosophy and the grandchild of religion.

Science and religion, however, are concerned with different dimensions of life. Ancient religions regarded natural and social phenomena as manifestations of a god's will and wisdom. But as science advanced, their doctrines were proven invalid in their approach to nature and human affairs, and they were discarded as they became increasingly ineffective in explaining the real phenomena of the universe.

In ancient India, philosophy and science advanced simultaneously. In that environment, Buddhism appeared. The truth which Shakyamuni Buddha realized intuitively is not the entirety of Buddhism. The Buddha and his followers explained the truth from various angles and gave it a systematic philosophical basis. That is how Buddhism was formally established as a religion. Nichiren Daishonin, the Buddha of the Latter Day of the Law, substantiated Shakyamuni's enlightenment and completed the system of philosophy and practice expounded by Buddhism.

18. The Compatibility of Science and Religion

IN the West, science and religion have long been considered incompatible. This has resulted in serious disputes, especially in the period since the beginning of the Christian era. Buddhism becomes that much more impressive when it becomes apparent that it poses no contradiction to scientific fact. This is partly because the realm which Buddhism opens and elucidates is of a completely different dimension than that of science.

Science investigates the phenomenal world in which human beings live and act, dealing with the objectively perceptible aspects of existence. The material aspect is only part of reality's entirety, yet physical phenomena are the most accessible to objective measurement and correlation. For this reason, the natural sciences advanced earlier than the other fields of science. Social phenomena were studied and examined, resulting in the development of the social sciences. Toward the end of the nineteenth century, human affairs became a major object of study and later resulted in great advances in the cultural sciences. Going further, the study of the human mind progressed from superstition and supposition to verifiable fact and substantiated theory.

The realms of what we call "science" are gradually

widening, but since the "scientific approach" is based on methodical, objective observation and reasoning, it is limited by its own nature. There are realms which are out of the reach of scientific cognition. Such realms can be grasped, if at all, only by the subjective and intuitive mind. This approach is more often applied to social phenomena than to nature, and more to the study of the human mind than to that of society. Buddhism elucidates truths based on one's subjective capacities, thereby drawing out the practical wisdom of life.

In its search for truth, science draws on mainly analytical and inductive reasoning, while Buddhist reasoning is a comprehensive method of deduction and intuition.

In order to lead better lives, objective cognition is necessary but not entirely effective. Science plays a powerful role in objective cognition, but how effectively this method is used to improve people's lives is decided by the degree to which individuals are awakened to the truth in the depths of their lives. This truth is what Buddhism elucidates. In this sense, science and religion are actually complementary to each other. In the words of Dr. Einstein, "Religion without science is blind; science without religion is lame."

Part Two
Buddhist Philosophy of Life

1. Outline

WHAT is Buddhism? The Lotus Sutra gives the clearest possible answer—it is a philosophy of life. More specifically, Buddhism teaches one how to purify one's life, develop the wisdom to grasp life's truth and establish true independence.

In the millennia since the death of Shakyamuni Buddha, his teachings were recorded and transmitted, giving rise to a bewildering array of sutras. Yet when one recognizes that the Lotus Sutra is the heart of them all, one sees that together they form what is actually a voluminous elucidation of the philosophy of life. Taken individually, however, the Buddhist sutras present many apparent mysteries. Some, for example, put forth monastic rules of discipline that strictly delineate correct behavior, while others recount stories from the unimaginably remote past as though they happened yesterday. According to some sutras, countless Buddhas and bodhisattvas of the distant past, as well as from the far reaches of the universe, gathered together where

Shakyamuni was expounding his teachings to his disciples.

Some also describe a certain world tens of thousands of light-years from the earth as clearly as though projected on a screen, or hold that one bodhisattva went underground to see his mother in a past existence. Many more parables and inconceivable events are depicted in the sutras. The great number of Buddhist scriptures preached by Shakyamuni are filled with mysteries, like a huge jungle with no trails.

Wandering into this dense forest of Buddhist doctrines, many Buddhists became utterly confused. They were forced to settle on one sutra or another, though they had only partial information and did not know exactly where they stood or where they were going. That is why such a large number of conflicting interpretations and schools arose along with the spread of Shakyamuni's teachings in India, Tibet, China, Japan, Burma, Thailand—all the countries that were touched by Buddhism.

However, Shakyamuni himself left a guidepost to lead the people to his true intentions. In the Lotus Sutra and its prologue, the *Muryōgi* Sutra (Sutra of Infinite Meaning), it is stated that the Lotus Sutra reveals the ultimate truth of Shakyamuni's enlightenment and is supreme among all his teachings. Nonetheless, many people overlooked this out of carelessness, or perhaps from lack of knowledge, and as a result they strayed by the wayside.

At various times in history Buddhist scholars, such as Nāgārjuna, Vasubandhu, T'ien-t'ai and Dengyō, realized that the Lotus Sutra is the most profound of all Shakyamuni's teachings. They found that the Lotus Sutra gives meaning to all the others. It integrates partial truths into an overall picture, and all of Shakyamuni's doctrines into a far-reaching philosophical system. This is what is called the philosophy of life.

What then did Shakyamuni want to impart through the Lotus Sutra? His enlightenment was his realization of the one truth underlying all life. Not only Shakyamuni, but Shāriputra, Mahākāshyapa and other disciples also attained enlightenment through this truth. It was, is and will always be the only road to enlightenment for all the Buddhas in the universe. In short, people can reach Buddhahood only by realizing the existence of this truth.

This truth is the eternal Law existing in and behind the phenomenal changes in the universe and pervading the boundless expanses of space. This is also the fundamental Law that operates within the depths of each individual life. Life has an infinite variety of manifestations and functions, but the entity or Law of life permeates all phenomena. Buddhist scriptures other than the Lotus Sutra are only partial and relative explanations of the fundamental Law of life.

Buddhism classifies life's ever-changing conditions into ten categories or states of existence. This concept is called the Ten Worlds. Hell is the state in which one is swayed by the impulse to destroy, and to ruin everyone, including oneself. Hunger is the state of insatiable desire, and in Animality one's actions are toward self-preservation and immediate profit, lacking any self-control. When one is egotistic and driven by the competitive spirit to dominate, one is in a state of Anger.

The next category, Humanity, is a tranquil state in which one controls one's desires or impulses through reason, and the state of Heaven is the joy one experiences from the satisfaction of a desire or a victorious struggle. Both arise from a relationship between life and the external factors surrounding it. For this reason, when the balance in life is disturbed, calmness and contentment inevitably plunge into the trouble-filled state of Hell, Hunger, Animality or Anger.

Buddhism works to awaken people to the ultimate reality of life lying below desires and impulses, so that they can consciously maintain balance in their lives. In some cases people grasp for this reality through the teachings of their predecessors, and in others they attempt to realize it intuitively by observing nature's phenomena. The state of life of the former is called Learning; for the latter, it is Realization.

Learning and Realization come about when one consciously attempts to realize the ultimate truth of life. However, if efforts are directed only toward self-improvement, any truth obtained will never be more than partial. Each form of life is inseparably linked with all other beings and things in the universe because the ultimate reality of life which supports them all is one with the life of the universe. Consequently, in the attempt to grasp an overall and complete view of life's truth, people must first realize that they cannot exist apart from other living beings, and then they must identify with the pain of others to the point that they exert themselves fully to relieve those around them of their sufferings. The ninth state, Bodhisattva, is the expression of total devotion to aiding and assisting others. It indicates a life filled with compassion. The highest state, Buddhahood, is reached when one has the wisdom to realize the essence of one's own life and that of others, that it continues in perfect harmony with the rhythm of the universe and exists from the infinite past to the eternal future.

The sutras other than the Lotus Sutra regarded the Ten Worlds as separate and independent of each other, not as interrelated parts of a whole entity. There was no systematic explanation of the Ten Worlds. In contrast, through the Lotus Sutra one can see that each of the ten states includes all of the ten within it and that a person has the potential to manifest all of the ten states. Moreover, one universal rule regulates their changing aspects. This rule, the ten factors of life, is applicable to all the Ten Worlds at any moment and is common to each entity of life. The ten factors are mentioned in the *Hōben* (second) chapter of the Lotus Sutra, and consist of appearance, nature, entity, power, influence, internal cause, relation, latent effect, manifest effect and consistency from beginning to end of all the nine factors. While the Ten Worlds express the differences among life's phenomena, the ten factors describe the pattern of existence common to all changing phenomena.

Life manifests itself in differing ways and thus reveals its distinctive character. Because each form of life has its own unique qualities, the two concepts of the Ten Worlds and the ten factors alone are not sufficient to perceive life in its entirety. The three realms of existence, which are also expounded in the Lotus Sutra, are necessary for a full expression of life. They are the realm of the five components, the realm of living beings and the realm of the environment. In the natural environment, such as air, land, the sea, rivers and the sun's rays, living beings of a particular species assist each other and cooperate with other forms of life in the struggle to survive. As they grow, living beings influence and incorporate their surroundings both spiritually and physically. They take on distinctions in accord with the peculiarities of their environment. The theory of the three realms was expounded to analyze and understand the individualization in life.

The preceding doctrines, which are revealed by Shakyamuni's sutras, are not always written in language clear enough for everyone to comprehend. It took a philosopher and master of Buddhism like the Great Teacher T'ien-t'ai (Chih-i) in China to understand these principles through extensive study and deep insight and then incorporate them into the system of philosophy which is called *ichinen sanzen* (three thousand realms in a single moment of life).

His achievements had great influence on Buddhist thought in China and Japan. However, T'ien-t'ai's Buddhism was far too difficult to be readily communicated to the majority of the people. In order to comprehend it, one needed unusual intelligence as well as an all-around knowledge of the Buddhist scriptures and theories formulated by such scholars as Nāgārjuna. As a result, T'ien-t'ai's philosophy, although deeply revealing about life, awoke little real appreciation of Buddhism in the people.

Most people, including even learned monks, were confused by allegorical doctrines describing the occult powers of the Buddhas and bodhisattvas. They were so misled that they could only hold Buddhism in blind awe. Some built up hopes for salvation through involved esoteric Buddhist rituals. For them, Buddhism was only a ship to take them completely away from the harsh realities of worldly sufferings and beyond to the shores of nirvana.

The true teachings of Buddhism, however, are not escapist or otherworldly. Basic to them is the idea that by realizing and grasping the ultimate truth inherent within one's own life one can act fearlessly and vigorously, and at the same time understand that all life, including one's own, is most sacred. It is much to be regretted that this essential spirit was lost in the confusing phraseology. Even today it remains obscured to the great majority of the people of the world.

Nichiren Daishonin, born in Japan in 1222, gave concrete and practical expression to the Buddhist philosophy of life that Shakyamuni taught and T'ien-t'ai illuminated. It was thereby brought into sharp focus and made relevant to people's daily lives. His achievement was like that of someone who renders a complex scientific theory into practical applications. It was like a work of art that expresses the great spirit of the artist and the philosophy of his age, giving it the power to directly affect and move the people who experience it.

2. *Ichinen Sanzen*

THOUGH the term *ichinen sanzen* has already appeared, the full extent of its meaning may not be clear. It is actually the name of a system of thought in itself, developed by T'ien-t'ai on the basis of the principles of life expounded by Shakyamuni, especially those in the Lotus Sutra. *Ichinen sanzen* is, therefore, the basic Buddhist life philosophy. *Ichinen* indicates the entity of life and *sanzen* signifies the varying aspects and phases it assumes. T'ien-t'ai included all life's phenomena into this single system, *ichinen sanzen*. The expression *sanzen* (three thousand) is an integration of the Ten Worlds, their mutual possession, the ten factors and the three realms of existence. These figures multiplied ($10 \times 10 \times 10 \times 3$) yield three thousand.

How much is really known about life? To a certain extent the functions and phenomena of an individual life can be charted through the sciences of biology, biochemistry and physiology, which analyze the physical parts of a living organism and shed light on their operation as a whole. On the other hand, psychology and psychiatry are studies of the human mind and its activities, both internally and in relation to its surroundings. All such physical or mental activities are functions of life, not life itself. The entity of life itself is beyond the comprehension of any science or system of logic.

Shakyamuni explained the ultimate reality of life in the *Muryōgi* Sutra through the so-called thirty-four negatives: "His body neither existing nor not existing, . . . neither square or round, . . . neither blue or yellow, . . . "* The same sutra reads, "Infinite meaning comes from the one Law," signifying that all phenomena are manifestations of the ultimate reality of life.

The Buddha is one who comprehends the ultimate reality of life. The wisdom to grasp the ultimate reality is called Buddha wisdom. The *Hōben* (second) chapter of the Lotus Sutra reads, "The wisdom of all Buddhas is infinitely profound and immeasurable." It is the wisdom to realize life in its entirety.

Myoho-renge-kyo means the entity of life itself, and Nam-myoho-renge-kyo indicates the entity of life in terms of its relationship with the three thousand changing conditions of all phenomena. In other words, the ultimate reality endowed with the three thousand aspects characterizing all phenomena is conversely Nam-myoho-renge-kyo.

3. Ten Worlds

THE Ten Worlds (*jikkai*) indicate ten states which a single entity of life manifests in the course of the flow of time. The major factor in the postulation of the

*". . . his body neither existing nor not existing, neither caused or conditioned, neither self or other, neither square or round, neither short or long, neither appearing or disappearing, neither born or extinguished, neither created or arising, neither acted or made, neither sitting or lying down, neither walking or standing, neither moving or turning, neither idle or still, neither advancing or retreating, neither in safety or danger, neither right or wrong, neither gaining or losing, neither that or this, neither departing or coming, neither blue or yellow, neither red or white, neither crimson or purple or any other sort of color, . . ." In the grammar of the Chinese text, this passage is expressed with a total of thirty-four negatives.

Ten Worlds is the subjective sensation experienced by the "self" in the depths of an individual life.

(1) The state of Hell (*jigoku*): In his treatise "The True Object of Worship," Nichiren Daishonin states, "Rage is the world of Hell."* This is a condition in which one is swayed by the impulse of rage to destroy and bring ruin upon oneself and others. Briefly, this state is represented by extreme suffering and despair.

(2) The state of Hunger (*gaki*): The same treatise reads, "Greed is the world of Hunger." This is a condition dominated by endless selfish desires for wealth, fame or pleasure in which one is never truly satisfied.

(3) The state of Animality (*chikushō*): In the same treatise it reads, "Foolishness is the world of Animality." In this condition one follows the pull of desires and instincts, lacking the wisdom to control oneself.

(4) The state of Anger (*shura*): "Perversity is the world of Anger." Conscious of one's self but egotistic, one cannot grasp things as they are, and disregards and violates the dignity of others.

(5) The state of Humanity (*nin*): "The True Object of Worship" says, "Calmness is the world of Humanity." This is the state in which one can temporarily control one's desires and impulses with reason. One lives a peaceful life in harmony with one's surroundings and other people.

(6) The state of Heaven (*ten*): "Joy is the world of Heaven." This is a condition of contentment and joy which one feels when released from suffering or upon satisfaction of some desire.

(7) The state of Learning (*shōmon*): The six condi-

*Major Writings, vol. 1, p. 52.

tions, from Hell through Heaven, are brought about by impulses or desires, but they are completely controlled by the restrictions placed on them by one's surroundings and are extremely vulnerable to changing circumstances. Learning, on the other hand, is a condition experienced when one strives toward a lasting state of contentment and stability through self-reformation and development. Concretely, *shōmon* is the state in which one dedicates oneself to creating a better life by learning from the ideas, knowledge and experiences of one's predecessors and contemporaries.

(8) The state of Realization (*engaku*): This condition is similar to Learning in that both indicate striving for self-reformation.[1] However, what distinguishes Realization from the condition of Learning is that instead of trying to learn from the achievements of one's predecessors, one tries to learn the way to self-reformation through direct observation of phenomena.

(9) The state of Bodhisattva (*bosatsu*): This is a state of compassion in which an individual devotes himself to the happiness of others even if he must make sacrifices. The people of Learning or Realization tend to lack compassion, going to extremes in the pursuit of their own self-perfection. A bodhisattva, in contrast, finds that the way to self-perfection lies only in the act of compassion—saving other people from their suffering.

(10) The state of Buddhahood (*butsu*): This condition is reached when one gains the wisdom to realize the ultimate reality of one's own life, the infinite compassion to direct one's activities constantly toward benevolent goals, a perfected eternal self, and total purity of life which nothing can corrupt. Buddhahood is an

ideal state which one can attain through Buddhist practice. Since no life-condition is static, Buddhahood cannot be thought of as a final goal; rather, it is a condition
that one experiences in the depths of one's being as one
continues to act with benevolence in everyday life. In
other words, Buddhahood appears in everyday life as
the actions of a bodhisattva—good deeds or compassionate acts.[2]

1. The treatise reads, "The fact that all things in this world
are transient is perfectly clear to us" (*Major Writings,* vol. 1,
pp. 52–53). This statement characterizes both Learning and
Realization in which one tries to seek something eternal by
awakening to the impermanence of all phenomena and the
instability of the six conditions of life from Hell to Heaven,
or the six paths. Even though one aims at the four noble
worlds (from Learning to Buddhahood), that does not mean
that one separates oneself from the six lower conditions.
Learning, Realization, Bodhisattva and Buddhahood all indicate one's will and efforts to reform oneself while remain-
ing in a society and civilization filled with the suffering and
evil of the six paths. Therefore, those in the state of Learning are not only scholars and the like; those in the state of
Realization are not limited to artists, philosophers, etc. Feeling delight with the simple pursuit of truth in society and
natural phenomena, even scholars can be said to be experiencing the state of Heaven. This also holds true with philosophers or artists. When artists feel delight in their pursuit
of beauty, they are experiencing the state of Heaven. When,
through pursuit of learning or art, however, they glance
inward at the depths of their own lives and take a step toward
comprehending their inner life, they are experiencing the

state of Learning or Realization. As such, these two conditions can be egotistic and closed, as long as they are only directed toward one's own reformation and perfection. On the other hand, when, through the pursuit of art and learning, scholars or artists devote themselves to helping others overcome their suffering and give them courage to live, enabling them to experience the joy of life, they are actually in the state of Bodhisattva.

2. Four basic characteristics of Buddhahood are represented by the four leaders of the Bodhisattvas of the Earth—Bodhisattvas Jōgyō (Superior Conduct), Muhengyō (Limitless Conduct), Jyōgyō (Pure Conduct) and Anryūgyō (Conduct of Standing Firm). That is, these four bodhisattvas correspond to the four virtues—true self, eternity, purity and happiness. The virtue of Jōgyō can be thought of as the absolute and indestructible integrity of one's self. Bodhisattva Muhengyō stands for the state of unlimited freedom through all eternity. Jyōgyō indicates the absolute purity of life in which the evil or egotistic nature is driven into a latent, unexpressed state. Anryūgyō represents a happy and pleasant life of complete fulfillment.

Nichiren Daishonin is the original Buddha who has eternally been enlightened to the ultimate truth or the Mystic Law since the infinite past of *kuon ganjo*. However, his behavior was that of Bodhisattva Jōgyō, the leader of the Bodhisattvas of the Earth. In a broader sense, all people who practice with firm faith in the Daishonin's Buddhism behave as the Bodhisattvas of the Earth, but are in reality children of the Buddha.

4. Mutual Possession of the Ten Worlds

THE mutual possession of the Ten Worlds is a somewhat difficult but important concept, meaning basically
that each of the ten states of life contains the potentials
of expressing itself and the other nine as well. The
sutras expounded before the Lotus Sutra maintained
that the Ten Worlds were viewed as distinct physical
places, each with its own particular inhabitants. For
example, Vasubandhu's *Kusha ron* (A Treasury of Analyses of the Law) states that Hell exists one thousand
yojana under the ground (one *yojana* is the distance that
a royal army was thought to march in a day—about
twenty-four kilometers according to one source). The
Shōbōnen Sutra (Sutra of Meditation on the True Law)
states that the world of Hunger exists five hundred
yojana beneath the earth. Those beings in Animality
(sentient beings other than humans) live in the water,
on the land and in the air. Those in Anger dwell in the
sea. Those in Humanity dwell on the earth, and those in
Heaven, in a palace or above a mountain. Those in
Learning and Realization live in the Land of Transition.
Bodhisattvas live in the Land of Actual Reward, and the
Buddhas, in the Land of Eternally Tranquil Light.

In contrast, the Lotus Sutra rejects the idea that the
Ten Worlds are separate from each other. The fact that
during the preaching of the Lotus Sutra the inhabitants
of the Ten Worlds all gathered together at the same
time is itself a negation of permanent independence of
any of the ten. The Lotus Sutra goes on to say that all
beings of the nine worlds possess the Buddha nature.

That is another way of saying that each and every person has the potential to attain Buddhahood.

In light of the Lotus Sutra, life is not fixed in one or another of the Ten Worlds but can manifest any of the ten, from Hell to Buddhahood, at any given moment. For a person in the condition of Hell his surroundings seem miserable, no matter where he is. For another experiencing Heaven the same surroundings are filled with happiness. If the Ten Worlds indicated places where people live, those in Hell would never be able to depart from suffering as long as they stayed there. On the contrary, when the Ten Worlds were shown to mean conditions of life, it became clear that those in the condition of Hell could also experience joy. The mutual possession of the Ten Worlds indicates the ever-present possibility of transition from one condition to another.

Observing a person's life for a certain period, one can see a basic tendency or a strong inclination toward one or more of the ten states. A compassionate individual's life is centered upon the condition of Bodhisattva. Yet even one whose basic life-tendency is Bodhisattva may manifest Hunger, Heaven, or some other condition at any moment. Thus, the condition of Bodhisattva, or any other, contains the potential to experience all the other conditions of life.

The term "human revolution" indicates the gradual elevation in the state which forms one's basic tendency and the establishment of Buddhahood as the basis of one's life. When, as a consequence of such elevation, one's life-activities center around the highest possible state, that of Buddhahood, then one has attained enlightenment.

5. Ten Factors of Life

THE ten factors of life (*jūnyoze*) are set forth in the
Hōben (second) chapter of the Lotus Sutra: "The true
entity of all phenomena can only be understood and
shared between Buddhas. This reality consists of the
appearance, nature, entity, power, influence, internal
cause, relation, latent effect, manifest effect, and their
consistency from beginning to end." Universal phenomena include all the states of life, from Hell to Buddhahood. This principle, the ten factors, is an analysis of
the unchanging aspects of life common to all changing
phenomena. *Nyoze* (literally, like this or as it is) indicates
the universal truth pervading all phenomena. Hence
both Hell and Buddhahood, different as they are, have
the ten factors in common. While the Ten Worlds
express the differences among phenomena, the ten factors describe the pattern of existence common to all
phenomena which the entity of life manifests at each
moment. These common factors give us a way to
understand how our life changes from one state to another and the true entity of life as revealed within the
changing aspects of the Ten Worlds. T'ien-t'ai of China
used this passage in the Lotus Sutra concerning the ten
factors as his scriptural authority for establishing the
doctrine of *ichinen sanzen*. Briefly, the meaning of the
ten factors of life is as follows:

(1) Appearance (*nyozesō*): The phenomenal and material aspects of life. From the concept of the three
truths (*see* p. 62), this corresponds to the truth of temporary existence (*ketai*).

(2) Nature (*nyozeshō*): The inherent disposition or quality that cannot be perceived directly from the outside. This corresponds to the truth of non-substantiality (*kūtai*).

(3) Entity (*nyozetai*): The entity of life which permeates and integrates appearance and nature. The entity per se is not visible, but one can observe the way it manifests itself through its physical appearance and inner nature. This corresponds to the truth of the Middle Way (*chūtai*).

(4) Power (*nyozeriki*): Life's inherent strength or energy to achieve something.

(5) Influence (*nyozesa*): The movement or action produced when latent energy is activated.

(6) Internal cause (*nyozein*): The cause latent in life which produces an effect of the same nature as itself, good or evil. Each internal cause simultaneously contains a latent effect.

(7) Relation (*nyozeen*): Also translated as external cause. Relation is not the environment itself but the function relating life to its surroundings. When activated by an external influence, an internal cause undergoes a change and simultaneously produces a new latent effect. It is also through the function of relation that latent effects become manifest. Relation can be viewed as the connection between life and outside influences through which one is able both to make causes and to experience their effects.

(8) Latent effect (*nyozeka*): The effect produced in the depths of life when an internal cause is activated by "relation." Since both internal cause and latent effect are dormant within life, they exist simultaneously,

without the time gap that often occurs between an action and its manifest effect.

(9) Manifest effect (*nyozehō*): The concrete, perceivable result that emerges with the passing of time as a consequence of internal cause and latent effect, such as experiences of happiness or unhappiness, joy or sorrow.[1]

(10) Consistency from beginning to end (*nyoze hommatsu kukyōtō*): The integrating factor which unifies the other nine from "appearance" to "manifest effect" in every moment of life. Interrelated with each other, all of the nine factors comprise a harmonious entity, which characterizes life.

1. A brief example may help show the interrelatedness of power, influence, internal cause, relation, latent effect and manifest effect. In order to chant daimoku, life's inherent power, in this case, faith, is prerequisite. Through the function of one's mouth, lips and tongue, this inherent power manifests itself as the action of chanting daimoku. Through the connection established by the action of chanting daimoku to the Gohonzon (relation), one makes the cause for attaining Buddhahood, and simultaneously, the latent effect of attaining Buddhahood is produced. (In this case, one's faith in the Gohonzon which prompts one to chant may also be considered "internal cause.") Later, because of one's relationship with one's surroundings, i.e., the activities in the world and society, this latent effect brings about manifest rewards, such as achievements in work or harmony in one's family. Relation, or external cause, does not mean things of the external world, but life's ability to produce change through its relationship with the phenomena of the external world. It is life's function to assimilate outside phenomena.

As the above explanation shows, the first three factors—appearance, nature and entity—are phases of life itself as understood from a static viewpoint. However, these three factors are not located on the same plane. Appearance, life's physical aspects, and nature, life's spiritual aspects, cannot be combined to form life's entity. Life's entity actually supports and gives rise to one's physical and spiritual aspects. Appearance and nature are the manifestations of entity.

Power, influence, internal cause, relation, latent effect and manifest effect are the functions of life. However, these six factors are not on the same plane. Power is inherent in life. In contrast, the influence of power interacts directly with the outside. Internal cause and latent effect are inherent in life. In contrast, the reward of cause and effect is visibly manifest in the external world. Relation is the intermediary connecting the potential with the manifest. Consistency from beginning to end integrates all nine factors, explaining that when the first three factors are collectively defined as entity (beginning) and the following six factors as function (end), both beginning and end, or the entity of all phenomena and its functions, are inseparable.

6. Three Realms of Existence

ALL life consists of the ten factors and manifests the Ten Worlds. The principle of the three realms of existence (*san seken*) further analyzes life at three different levels and explains the distinctive character of individual life forms. The three realms are:

(1) The realm of the five components (*go'on seken*): An analysis of the functions of life in influencing and

assimilating its surroundings. The five components are
form, perception, conception, volition and consciousness. Form, or the physical aspect of life, includes everything that constitutes the body and its organs through
which one perceives the outer world. Perception means
the function of receiving or apprehending external
information through one's sense organs. Conception
indicates the function by which life grasps and forms
some idea or concept about what has been perceived.
Volition means the will to initiate some sort of action
following the creation of conceptions about some perceived object. Consciousness means the subjective
entity supporting and integrating the other four components, as well as the discerning function of life which
can make value judgments.

(2) The realm of living beings (*shujō seken*): The five
components of life unite temporarily to form an individual living being, who can experience Hell, Hunger,
and the other eight worlds. Moreover, no living being
exists in perfect isolation; all are in a state of constant
interrelationship and reciprocal influence with other
living beings. In this sense, the realm of living beings
can also be interpreted collectively as the social environment of an individual living being.

(3) The realm of the environment (*kokudo seken*):
Living beings invariably have some sort of environment, which in turn supports their existence.[1]

1. *Seken* of *san seken* means not only "realm" but "distinction."
The principle of the three realms (sometimes called the
three principles of individualization) also explains the unique
qualities which distinguish life's individual manifestations.

The most basic differences are those of the Ten Worlds. The five components of life, living beings and their environments all reflect the differences of these ten states. For example, someone in the state of Hell will perceive, form a conception of, and react to the same phenomenon in a completely different manner than someone in the state of Bodhisattva. Also, in terms of the Ten Worlds, differences in the environment do not mean differences in physical location, but rather, differences in the condition of the land. The condition of the land is a reflection of the life-condition of the people inhabiting it. According to the life-condition of the inhabitants, a land may at times manifest the state of Hell, Heaven and so on.

In addition to the fundamental differences of the Ten Worlds, one finds individual differences. The five components differ from one individual to another. For example, even among people with the same basic life-tendency of Learning, no two will have exactly the same physical form, and no two will perceive, conceive and react to their environment in exactly the same way. Similarly, no two people have exactly the same social or natural environments.

If one defines living beings, which consist of the five components, as *shōhō* (the entity) of *eshō funi* (the oneness of an entity and its surroundings), their natural environment is *ehō* (the surroundings). If one analyzes the individual living being further, its consciousness is *shōhō* and the other four of the five components—form or body, perception, conception and volition—work to make it interact with other living beings and the natural environment which together form *ehō*.

7. Three Truths

To the Buddhist, all things are "phenomena." All matter is nothing more than form, comprised of a union of its parts. For example, water has its own constituent elements, which under certain conditions combine to form a refreshing drink. It is now known that this view accords perfectly with the scientific fact that water is basically a combination of two hydrogen atoms and one oxygen atom per molecule.

Buddhism explains that all forms are comprised of constituent elements, which, uniting, give rise to phenomena, and separating, cause the dissolution of phenomena. Moreover, these elements themselves prove on analysis to have no fixed or absolute existence. This, too, accords with the findings of modern science. It follows that ultimately no phenomena in the world can be perfectly grasped according to currently prevailing concepts of "existence." For example, the bonding which enables molecules, atoms or nuclei to "exist" is something which itself does not fit within the category of existence. This is what the concept of non-substantiality (*kū*) means. All things are formed from elements that are ultimately non-substantial in nature and through bonding that is also non-substantial. These then appear as transient phenomena in the state of temporary existence (*ke*), or constant flux. However, non-substantiality and temporary existence are not contradictory concepts. The internal nature of a single phenomenon comes under the heading of *kū,* and its surface or visible aspects can be thought of as *ke*. All phenomena have the two aspects of non-substantiality and temporary existence. Even the most highly complex phenomenon of all, human life, is a temporary combination of basic elements which at their essence are in *kū,* the potential state that cannot be defined as either existence or nonexistence.

If one tries to grasp phenomena with just these two truths of non-substantiality and temporary existence, everything, including human life, appears transitory, with no absolute or fixed existence of its own. It seems that all the workings of the entire universe are mere happenstance. This presents a challenge to the prevailing perception of reality. According to the law of chance, it would be perfectly plausible for significant numbers of human beings to be born with three, four or even five arms. However, human beings have common qualities and characteristics unique to their species, which are clearly different from those of other living beings. The key to this selective differentiation is the concept of the Middle Way (*chū*).

The truth of the Middle Way is that all phenomena are characterized by both non-substantiality and temporary existence, yet are in essence neither. The Middle Way is the essence of continuity which is either manifest or latent. Together, temporary existence, non-substantiality and the Middle Way are called the three truths (*santai*), an effective means to understand accurately all phenomena in the universe.

8. The Three Bodies of a Buddha

THE concept of the three bodies of a Buddha (*sanjin*), or the three properties of a Buddha's life, is closely related to the three truths of non-substantiality, temporary existence and the Middle Way. By studying and understanding the Buddha's life in terms of the three truths, one gains an understanding of the three bodies. The sutras explain in many different ways how great the Buddha is. For instance, they list the Buddha's thirty-two features and eighty sublime characteristics. Such characteristics are naturally transitory and provisional. They are said to be possessed by the Buddha in accordance with the people's way of thinking in those days as a means to stimulate their aspiration toward the Buddha. The Buddha's physical aspect is called the manifested body, or the property of action (*ōjin, ō* meaning "compliance" with popular inclinations), in which he appears in this world in order to save the people. The physical property of the Buddha's life corresponds to the temporary existence of the three truths.

Another thing that the Buddhist scriptures explain is the superior wisdom possessed by the Buddha. Wisdom is not physical and therefore can be grasped only on the basis of the truth of non-substantiality. The Buddha wisdom is acquired through different experiences, and each Buddha therefore has his own characteristic wisdom as his reward for completing bodhisattva practices and thereby realizing the fundamental truth. Just as one person may have knowledge of medicine and another may be good at law, Buddhas each have their characteristic wisdom. Specialists acquire skill or knowledge through study; in the same way Buddhas develop their spiritual qualities as the effect of ceaseless effort and discipline. This spiritual aspect of the Buddha's life is called the bliss body, or the property of wisdom (*hōshin,* in which *hō* means reward).

The properties of action and wisdom, the Buddha's physical and spiritual "bodies," are functions of his life, but they are not its essence. The essence is called *hosshin* which means the Dharma body, or the property of the Law, and it corresponds to the Middle Way. Life's essential nature cannot be grasped in the context of either non-substantiality or temporary existence. The *Muryōgi* Sutra, the introduction to the Lotus Sutra, describes the essential nature of the Buddha's life through the use of thirty-four negatives* in order to show that it cannot be understood with ideas or expressed in terms ordinarily used to describe physical or spiritual phenomena.

These three bodies or properties can help us understand the Buddha's life, but they are integral aspects of one Buddha. A Buddha is invariably endowed with all three of them. Consequently, the Buddha is not just some abstract entity (*hosshin*) which is beyond one's understanding, but invariably appears as a real person with the compassionate actions (*ōjin*) and profound wisdom (*hōshin*) to attract people and lead them to the solutions to their sufferings in life. That is, the Buddha is not a theoretical existence but very much a human being—an enlightened human being.

*See footnote on p. 49.

9. Oneness of Body and Mind

PSYCHOSOMATIC medical treatment in the West is based
on relatively recent developments in science which
take into account the relationship between mind and
body in physical illnesses. In Buddhism the relationship
of body and mind has long been understood to be inseparable; this concept is indicated in the term *shikishin
funi*. *Shiki* means matter and all physical phenomena
including the human body. *Shin* means spiritual phenomena and the workings of reason, sense, emotion
and volition. *Funi* is the abbreviation of *nini-funi,* which
literally means "two but not two." This seemingly contradictory phrase becomes clear when it is rendered
as "two in phenomena but not two in essence."

Though the material and the spiritual are two separate classes of phenomena, they are in essence indi-
visible. When a person becomes excited, his heart beats
faster than usual. Profound suffering or anguish causes
one's life force to weaken, while a life rich with vitality
refreshes both body and mind. Accordingly, delicate
changes in one's mental or emotional state emerge to
the surface and are reflected in one's facial expressions,
or some other part of the body, thus becoming discern-
ible.

This much can be understood, but it still conveys
only a small part of the concept of the oneness of body
and mind. Matter and spirit are equally basic, united as
an inseparable whole, the function of which is to spon-
sor life-activity. Life is never manifest without both.
This concept explains life in terms of the unity of life's

two aspects, and conveys more profoundly the nature of phenomenal life in its relation to the ultimate reality. The distinction between material and spiritual pertains to the level of phenomena, and their essential oneness, to that of the ultimate reality of life. Nichiren Daishonin states in the "Ongi kuden" (Record of the Orally Transmitted Teachings): "The supreme principle reveals that the physical and the spiritual are one and inseparable within the ultimate reality of life."* The oneness of body and mind is an expression of the ultimate reality of life. To try to understand the oneness of body and mind apart from the reality of life is to misunderstand it completely.

In interpreting the relationship of body and mind from the standpoint of the three truths, physical phenomena correspond to temporary existence (*ke*), and spiritual phenomena, to non-substantiality (*kū*). Moreover, the essential reality of life, the oneness of the spiritual and the physical, can be grasped through the perception of the Middle Way (*chū*). This relationship is also explained in terms of the three bodies, or properties of the Buddha's life.

10. Existence and Essence

WHAT are the Buddhist views on existence and essence? To begin with, essence is not separated from existence, nor is it merely the product of human imagi-

Nichiren Daishonin gosho zenshū (hereafter cited as *Gosho zenshū*), p. 708.

nation. Essence is integral within existence, and there
can be no essence apart from existence. Generally, existence can be defined as a manifestation of some form
that essence assumes. Essence invariably takes on a
form or physical aspect, and thus existence contains
both phases of form and essence. These three exist as a
unified whole. This idea is represented by the concept
of the unification of the three truths. The truth of non-
substantiality is the perception of essence or the spiritual aspect. The truth of temporary existence relates to
form or the physical aspect, and the truth of the Middle
Way encompasses the concept of existence or the true
entity of a given phenomenon. To try to understand the
universe on the basis of only one of these three would
be incomplete, for no single truth can provide a perfect
understanding of existence. Only by combining all
three truths is it possible to grasp the true entity of life.
Buddhism expounds the unification of the three truths,
a principle that sets forth the mutually inclusive relationship of entity, form and essence. The coexistence of
entity, form and essence may appear to contradict the
idea of eternal life. This question is important when one
attempts to understand the state in which one's life will
continue.

After death, life does not go somewhere else, nor
does it continue its existence as a "soul." A single life is
ultimately one with universal life, which means that it
extends throughout the universe. One's life is not confined to one's body but exists within and beyond one's
body in infinite expansion. The concept of the three
realms of existence, one component of the theory of
ichinen sanzen, includes the realm of the five compo-

nents which constitute a living being, the realm of living beings who are integrated individuals capable of interacting with their surroundings, and the realm of the environment, or the place where living beings carry out their life-activities. It embraces the idea that a single entity of life can pervade society and the whole universe, and that it lives and carries out its activities in the boundless expanses of space.

Death is a temporary discontinuance of the functions that make up and maintain an individual life, but it is not the extinction of life itself. Because the functions of an individual life are discontinued, it ceases to exist as a separate and independent organism, and instead life in the state one calls death fuses into the environment and the universe and unites with them. Rather, even while alive, a life continues on eternally with its own unique personality in perfect fusion with the universe. The merging of an individual life with the universe is like the subsiding of a wave in the sea. Death becomes the merging of the individual and the universal. When a life is united with the universe, it is but one cycle in a chain of a continual existence extending from the infinite past to the eternal future. This cycle repeats the process of unification and separation, or individualization, over and over again. In the process of unification, an entity, its form and essence merge as an integral whole with the universal life and, in the process of individualization, all three come forth again as a single being.

11. Life and Its Environment

THE relationship between human life and its environment is explained in terms of *eshō funi,* the oneness of life and its environment. *Eshō* is a contraction of the Japanese terms *ehō* and *shōhō. Ehō* indicates the insentient environment or objective world, and *shōhō,* the living self or subjective world. The syllable *hō* here means manifest effect, or the results of karma. The effects of an individual living being's past karma manifest themselves in both its subjective life and its objective environment.

Since *funi* means "two in phenomena but not two in essence," *eshō funi* means that life and its environment are two distinct phenomena but one in their fundamental essence. People and their environment are inseparable, but *eshō funi* as a concept goes further than denoting just the inseparable relationship between the two.

Many people today feel somehow out of kilter with their environment, which seems to result only in unhappiness. But it is humankind as a whole that has gone against the rhythm of the natural world, polluting it and causing stress that has just begun to manifest its consequences in the environment. The oneness of life and its environment is a principle that suggests how people can influence and reform their environment through inner change, or the elevation of their state of life. Contained within is the idea that just as the environment influences the individual, the individual also can effect change in the environment.

Ideally, human beings should live in harmony with their environment. One creates one's own unique existence in accordance with the laws of individualization, and one shapes a unique environment compatible to oneself. But the formation of one's environment must coincide with the emergence of one's life in this world; a person cannot appear without an environment, simply floating in space. Each of us has an environment, however, and each of us is essentially distinct, so we all relate to our surroundings differently. The way we see the environment differs depending on our state of life and our circumstances.

An environment is a reflection of the inner life of the individual living within it; it takes on characteristics which accord with the life-condition of the individual in question. In other words, life extends its influence into the surroundings.

The principle of *ichinen sanzen* includes the oneness of life and its environment. In terms of the three realms of existence, *shōhō* corresponds to the realms of the five components and of living beings, and *ehō,* to the realm of the environment. The consciousness of the individual living being may be described as *shōhō,* and the other four of the five components—form or body, perception, conception and volition—exist to make the individual interact with other living beings and the natural environment, which together form *ehō. Ichinen sanzen* reveals that both *shōhō* and *ehō* are inherent in a single moment of life. Thus Buddhism views life as comprising a vast expanse of influence and activity that integrates both living beings and their surroundings.

12. Enlightenment in Insentient Beings

ALL existence can be broadly classified as either sentient or insentient beings. As the term suggests, sentient beings have, through the functioning of their central nervous system, the ability to sense, that is, to feel, think, desire and love. Insentient beings lack such capacities. They can, nevertheless, manifest the state of enlightenment, or Buddhahood. But the way insentient beings attain Buddhahood is quite different from the way human beings attain this state.

Developing Buddhahood in one's life calls for a strong determination to make constant efforts toward growth and self-development. Insentient beings, lacking the mental functions required for this, cannot spontaneously struggle to achieve self-development.

But Buddhist thought holds that life and its environment are inseparable. A mutual relationship of supporting, nurturing and influencing exists between sentient and insentient beings. Thus both may be viewed as being essentially one. The attainment of Buddhahood, therefore, cannot be restricted to sentient beings alone.

In fact, Buddhism expounds two types of enlightenment for insentient beings. The first is derived from the principle that all things in the universe, sentient and insentient, possess the potential to attain Buddhahood. The second refers to situations in which objects such as paper and wood can be made to reveal the state of Buddhahood. The latter case occurs in connection with the object of worship.

The object of worship should be the Buddha's life

itself, and in the Latter Day of the Law this signifies the life of the original Buddha, Nichiren Daishonin. When the Daishonin carried out his mission by inscribing his life on a block of camphorwood in the form of the Dai-Gohonzon, he infused the insentient piece of wood with his life of Buddhahood. This is the object of worship to lead all humankind in the Latter Day of the Law to enlightenment.

In accordance with the principle of the oneness of life and its environment, when a sentient being attains Buddhahood, the same state of life will be simultaneously manifested in the insentient beings of its surroundings. For example, when sentient beings who have attained Buddhahood see a mountain, the mountain appears to them as the entity of Buddhahood. However, when other sentient beings in the world of Hunger see the same mountain, it appears to them as the entity of Hunger. Insentient beings do not have the capacity to develop themselves. If they are to attain Buddhahood, there must be a sentient being who will act upon them, thereby allowing them to manifest their innate Buddha nature.

Both mountains and seas affect character development. The same can be said of works of art. Indeed, primitive peoples actually deified natural phenomena such as mountains and rivers. What makes the Gohonzon stand out in sharp contrast to other insentient beings is the attitude of the human beings who have a relationship with it.

For example, even if one observes a beautiful natural scenery and thinks to oneself, "How lovely!" one does not actually "believe" in it. The scene makes an impression that remains with one. Some people might even attempt to capture that impression in photographs or paintings. However, in the case of the Gohonzon, human beings have faith in it, and dedicate their lives to it. To the degree that they do so, the Gohonzon demonstrates great power. Without this kind of faith, the Gohonzon, even though it has the power to lead all living beings to Buddhahood, will not be able to show this power. The Gohonzon is the external cause. Faith is the internal cause. When external cause and internal cause are harmonized, one is able to display with great clarity the Buddha nature that exists within one's life.

13. Eternity of Life

THE eternity of life is a view that is certainly not unique to Buddhism; it was widely accepted among many of the ancient Indian religions. Buddhism discovered the law of cause and effect that works within and behind this eternal flow of life. However, this view is still based on fatalism or determinism, and virtually denies the existence of a free will. Delving deeper into the law of causation, the Lotus Sutra taught that people possess an inherent power with which to challenge fate and break its chains.

The causes one formed in the past bring about corresponding effects in the present, and one's actions in the present in turn shape one's future. Yet, as long as one's life in this world is predestined as the result of past causes, one cannot change one's individual destiny for

the better. Without going back to the past and changing one's past causes, one can do nothing but resign oneself to one's present circumstances. But it is impossible
to repeat the past, and thereby to change the present.
Such is the ordinary view of destiny.

In contrast to this, the Lotus Sutra elucidated the
reality of the eternal and unchangeable life which exists
independently of karma that has been created according to the law of causality, and taught that it is possible
to change one's destiny as well as the future by bringing
forth this life from within. In order to make people
understand this, the Lotus Sutra, through a detailed
analysis of life, clarified the system of life and the law by
which it functions.

The concept of the eternity of life cannot be readily
understood by contemporary people, although it was
an integral part of ancient Indian religions. It is one of
the most controversial issues. Moreover, the eternity of
life is nearly impossible to verify scientifically. If scien-
tists wish to analyze the state in which life continues
after physical death, they must first grasp what life
really is. But there are still no scientific methods with
which to grasp the essential quality of life itself.

Religious hypotheses must be judged on how well
they explain the phenomenon of life, which seems
inexplicable to the unaided human intelligence. The
Buddhist concept that life is eternal and yet undergoes
constant change from one form to another is the most
sound explanation to account for the differences in the
various fates of human beings from the time they come
into the world. People are born into different circumstances and conditions, which they must challenge if

they are to achieve happiness. If a previous existence is not posited for a person living in the present, the fate or karma of that person must be ascribed either to an absolute, supernatural being, or to pure chance. Heredity alone cannot account for individual differences, for differences exist even among children of the same parents. In conclusion, the most reasonable explanation is that one's life continues on eternally, depending on the law of karma or cause and effect which operates over the past, present and future.

14. Nine Consciousnesses

IN Buddhist thought, the spiritual functions of perception or discernment are classified into nine. They are called the nine *vijñānas* or consciousnesses (*kushiki*). The first five consciousnesses correspond to the five senses of sight, hearing, smell, taste and touch.* The sixth to the ninth consciousnesses are the perceptive functions of the human mind. To perceive the entirety of the mind as possessing four particular functions may seem difficult to understand at first, but this approach actually shows the deep and far-reaching insight of Buddhism.

The sixth consciousness integrates the perceptions of the five senses into coherent images and makes judgments about the external world. For example, when

*Modern physiology has shown that each of the five sense organs (eyes, ears, nose, tongue and body) also involves the functions of perception and discernment, which proves that each of the five sense organs in itself possesses a consciousness as defined in Buddhism.

one comes into contact with a beautiful but bad-smell-ing object, one will naturally reject it. Such judgment is made by the sixth consciousness. All living beings which have a central nervous system, no matter how complex or simple they may be, possess this sixth con-sciousness.

The seventh consciousness is called *mano*-conscious-ness in Sanskrit, meaning the power of thinking and pondering. With abstract concepts or the systems of thought such as the view of life and the world, which are beyond the perceptions of the five sense organs, one reflects upon the way of one's existence and the mean-ing of phenomena associated with one's daily living, and behaves accordingly. This level of consciousness in-cludes awareness of and attachment to the self, as well as the capacity to distinguish between good and evil.

The eighth consciousness is called *ālaya*-conscious-ness. *Ālaya* means repository, and all the experiences of the present and previous lifetimes—karma—are stored there. All the actions and experiences of life that take place through the first seven consciousnesses are accu-mulated as karma in this *ālaya*-consciousness, which at the same time exerts an influence on the workings of the seven consciousnesses. The Freudian concept of the unconscious is somewhat similar to this. It stores up impressions perceived in the mind and simultaneously causes new mental actions. All actions of life coming under the law of causality stem from the realm of the eighth consciousness. This consciousness forms the framework of individual existence.

The ninth consciousness, the basis of all spiritual functions, is called *amala*-consciousness. *Amala* means pure or undefiled. Whereas the *ālaya*-consciousness contains karmic impurities, the *amala*-consciousness lies within the innermost depths of life and remains pure, free from all defilement from one's actions in a previous life. Nichiren Daishonin identified the ninth consciousness as Nam-myoho-renge-kyo, the fundamental Buddha nature extending from the infinite past to the infinite future.

15. Time without Beginning

KUON means infinite past, and *ganjo* means the beginning of all things. The phrase *kuon ganjo* may evoke some idea of creation as in the Judeo-Christian tradition, but in Buddhism there is no myth of creation nor any concept of an original beginning. According to the Buddhist view, the universe is itself an eternal existence without beginning or end. Its continuous flow remains uninterrupted, as seen in the ceaseless formation and collapse of stars and star clusters, and in the birth and death of living beings, including humans.

The concept of *kuon ganjo* was originally formed based on the *Juryō* (sixteenth) chapter of the Lotus Sutra. There Shakyamuni reveals that he attained Buddhahood in the remote past—*kuon* or *gohyaku-jintengō* —and that well before *gohyaku-jintengō* he had fulfilled the requisites of a bodhisattva to attain enlightenment. Both law and mentor are necessary to carry out these requisites, and so Shakyamuni himself must have studied under such a mentor. But he did not touch upon the exact definition of the law or reveal who his teacher in the inconceivably distant past was.

Nichiren Daishonin first made it clear that the law that Shakyamuni practiced was Nam-myoho-renge-kyo and that his mentor was the original Buddha who has enabled all Buddhas throughout time to attain enlightenment. Nichiren Daishonin called the original Buddha the "Buddha of *kuon ganjo*"* because this Buddha had already been enlightened in *kuon ganjo,* in a past far more distant than even the inconceivably remote past of *gohyaku-jintengō*. He also called Nam-myoho-renge-kyo the "Mystic Law of *kuon ganjo*."

In its true sense the concept of *kuon ganjo* does not mean just the infinite past; rather, it indicates a time without beginning, an eternity with neither beginning nor end, beyond the confines of time. In this sense eternity is the unbroken continuance of a single moment. Thus, the present moment or any moment contains the ultimate existence in which the past without beginning and the infinite future are both contained. *Kuon ganjo* therefore equals the present moment.

In each momentary existence of one's life there dwells Nam-myoho-renge-kyo, the ultimate reality of life. Although one accumulates many experiences, the essential reality of life neither disappears nor changes. Through the eternal cycle of birth and death, a person

*The Buddha of *kuon ganjo* can be defined as Nam-myoho-renge-kyo or the Mystic Law, that is, the life of the cosmos itself. This is the Buddha who directly reveals and himself embodies or personifies the Mystic Law. In contrast, the provisional Buddha is a provisional embodiment of the Mystic Law who does not clarify the cause that enabled him to attain his enlightenment. Viewed in the light of the Law of Nam-myoho-renge-kyo, Nichiren Daishonin is the manifestation of the Buddha of *kuon ganjo*.

accumulates a variety of karma. Yet even through this series of births and deaths, the essential reality of one's life never changes. It exists eternally. When, through one's faith in the Gohonzon, one draws forth the essential reality of Nam-myoho-renge-kyo from within the depths of one's life, one can return to one's original existence even within this lifetime. That is, one can return to the state of life that has existed within one since *kuon ganjo*. This is the Buddhist concept of the oneness of *kuon* or eternity and *mappō* (the Latter Day of the Law), the present moment, in which one is living. More concretely, by practicing and propagating Nam-myoho-renge-kyo in the context of this present time-space framework, human beings bring forth from within their lives the Buddha nature they have inherently possessed since time without beginning.

Part Three
Essence of the Lotus Sutra

1. The Lotus Sutra

HINAYANA Buddhism may be described as nihilistic because it expounds the senselessness and uselessness of life in this phenomenal world. Provisional Mahayana Buddhism, on the other hand, is similar to escapism in that it generally seeks happiness and meaning not in this but in some other world. The Lotus Sutra, true Mahayana Buddhism, is a dramatic contrast. It is a philosophy which reveals the key to reforming this world. In contrast to other philosophies or ideologies that advocate a reformation of external or social conditions, true Mahayana Buddhism leads toward a reformation within the human being himself. It is this spiritual revolution which produces a lasting, positive change in society and the whole environment. In other words, a true social revolution can only evolve on the basis of an individual human revolution.

The *Muryōgi* Sutra (Sutra of Infinite Meaning) and the *Fugen* Sutra (Sutra of Bodhisattva Fugen) are respectively the prologue and the epilogue to the Lotus Sutra. The *Muryōgi* Sutra explains that all principles and

81

meanings are born from a single Law. It also suggests that this single Law will be revealed in the Lotus Sutra. The *Fugen* Sutra states that inexhaustible and all-encompassing wisdom begins to function when a person is awakened to the one Law in the Lotus Sutra.

The Lotus Sutra itself consists of twenty-eight chapters. The first fourteen are called *shakumon,* or the theoretical teaching, and the latter fourteen are called *hommon,* or the essential teaching. *Hon* means a substantial body and *shaku,* shadow. *Mon* means teachings. The theoretical teaching takes the form of preaching by a provisional Buddha, the historical Shakyamuni Buddha who is depicted as having first attained enlightenment during this lifetime. It teaches that all kinds of life possess the capacity to understand the ultimate reality of life. It explains the possibility of attaining Buddhahood but does so only in theory without citing any concrete instance. Therefore, *shakumon* is a very general universal truth, but does not lead to accomplished fact. Hence its name, which implies the nature of a shadow.

By comparison, the essential teaching takes the form of preaching by the Buddha who discards his transient role as the historical Shakyamuni and reveals his true identity as the Buddha who attained enlightenment in the remote past of *gohyaku-jintengō.* It cites Shakyamuni's actual experience of enlightenment—when and how he realized the ultimate reality of life. Yet not even in this part of the Lotus Sutra did Shakyamuni clearly identify the ultimate reality of life. It is Nichiren Daishonin who clarified it and opened the way for all people to attain Buddhahood.

2. The *Hōben* and *Juryō* Chapters

THE Lotus Sutra consists of twenty-eight chapters, and among these the second or *Hōben* chapter and the sixteenth or *Juryō* chapter are especially important. The Lotus Sutra's preeminence among all the sutras lies in its assertion that all people can become Buddhas as Shakyamuni did, and in its philosophy which provides the theoretical explanation for this possibility.

In the *Hōben* chapter Shakyamuni begins to impart his enlightenment to his disciples. He reveals for the first time that all people have equal potential to attain Buddhahood. In the *Juryō* chapter he declares that he actually attained Buddhahood before this lifetime—in the distant past called *gohyaku-jintengō*. By showing his own Buddhahood to be of such long duration, he points to the Buddha nature eternally inherent in all human beings. Nichiren Daishonin taught that Nam-myoho-renge-kyo is the Law Shakyamuni revered in order to attain Buddhahood in the distant past. Reciting the *Juryō* chapter during gongyo is praising the great power of Nam-myoho-renge-kyo, the Law implied in this chapter, while reciting the *Hōben* chapter is expressing the belief that this power of Nam-myoho-renge-kyo, which is inherent in one's own life, will become manifest and lead one toward Buddhahood. With this expectation deep in one's heart one praises the supreme Law, Nam-myoho-renge-kyo.

Praising the Law, Nam-myoho-renge-kyo, is, at the same time, expressing gratitude to the Person, Nichiren

Daishonin. Reciting the *Juryō* chapter is an expression of gratitude to Nichiren Daishonin, who first revealed the Law of Nam-myoho-renge-kyo lying in the depths of this chapter, which is the teacher of all the Buddhas of past, present and future. Reciting the *Hōben* chapter, on the other hand, gives voice to one's awe and respect for the Daishonin as the Buddha who made it possible for people in the Latter Day of the Law to become Buddhas and to enjoy the same state of enlightenment as his own.

The *Hōben* and *Juryō* chapters are clearly the most important of the twenty-eight chapters of the Lotus Sutra, and that is why in the Gosho, Nichiren Daishonin exhorts believers to recite the *Hōben* and *Juryō* chapters and chant Nam-myoho-renge-kyo.

The word *hōben,* literally "expedient means," here indicates preparatory teachings which are meant to lead people to the true teaching. To illustrate, they function like a bus, car or train carrying people from home to school or office. If study or work is the destination, then *hōben* is the means of getting there. Since both study and work are vital if people are to improve life and be able to live a more truly human existence, these "means" are very important, indeed.

One reason the *Hōben* chapter is so called is because in it, Shakyamuni declares the preparatory nature of everything taught in the forty-two years before he expounded the Lotus Sutra. Everything was aimed only at leading people to the Lotus Sutra. This chapter is a statement, then, that the Lotus Sutra is the only true teaching. It is also called the *Hōben* chapter because it reveals that the life-activities of common mortals of the nine worlds (from Hell through Bodhisattva) are the means by which they manifest Buddhahood.

If, as the *Hōben* chapter shows, the Buddha nature is inherent in one's life and one is therefore a potential Buddha, then to manifest the Buddha nature is one's goal, and the states of the nine worlds are the means to attain it. For example, everyone has problems in daily life. They may be family troubles, difficulties at work, or sufferings stemming from character flaws. But when those problems compel one to pray to the Gohonzon, they become the means which lead to one's human revolution.

The meaning of *hōben* also applies to Shakyamuni's teaching in the Lotus Sutra itself. The sutra itself is basically a "means" leading to the ultimate truth, which is Nam-myoho-renge-kyo of the Three Great Secret Laws. Not even in the Lotus Sutra itself did Shakyamuni Buddha clearly reveal the Law to which he was enlightened.

Nichiren Daishonin revealed this ultimate truth in the Latter Day of the Law. Even then, from one perspective, what the Daishonin taught is still a means— the only means in the Latter Day—to attain enlightenment. Through faith, practice and study based on the Gohonzon, in which the Daishonin embodied his enlightenment, the truth may be experienced in the depths of one's being and made the basis of one's life. As Nichiren Daishonin wrote to Lady Nichinyo, "Never seek this Gohonzon outside yourself. The Gohonzon exists only within the mortal flesh of us ordinary people who embrace the Lotus Sutra and chant Nam-myoho-renge-kyo."*

So far means has been discussed, as distinct from end, truth or result. But there are also instances where the means is not only closely connected to the end but becomes the end itself. The purpose of participating in sports, for example, is not merely to win a gold medal. An even greater purpose is the strengthening of one's body and mind through the serious pursuit of sports. In this case, means and end are inseparable.

In Buddhism a preparatory teaching (means) which simultaneously contains the true teaching (end) is called *himyō hōben. Hi* means "hidden," that is, the truth hidden in the preparatory teachings; *myō* means "beyond conception" or "unfathomable." In this sense, the *hōben* or "means" referred to in the second chapter are both teachings preliminary to the truth and, looking more deeply, teachings containing the truth.

It may be helpful to reconsider what has been said so far about *hōben* in the light of *himyō hōben*. From this perspective, it is apparent that the sutras taught before the Lotus Sutra are not merely preparatory teachings set down to lead people to the true teaching, but each of them contains part of the truth. Yet even so, the entire truth is contained only in the Lotus Sutra. Only after grasping the truth in the Lotus Sutra can one go back to the pre-Lotus Sutra teachings and discern the important points within the partial truths they contain. When a part of the truth is seen in proper relation to the whole, it can be a trustworthy guide.

A similar relationship exists between Buddhahood

*Major Writings, vol. 1, p. 213.

and the other nine worlds. In a sense, the nine worlds are no more than a means to achieve the highest state of Buddhahood, but consider if the Buddha's life could exist without the nine worlds. Even to imagine such a possibility is to miss the whole point of the Lotus Sutra's teaching. There is no state of Buddhahood without the other nine worlds; they are necessary and integral components of life. As long as human beings are composed of flesh and blood, whether they are Buddhas or not, they will have the desires and instincts indispensable to their lives as men and women. They intrinsically possess all of the nine worlds, from Hell to Bodhisattva. The nine worlds are each distinct states, but they are also inseparable, and, when based on the Law of life, Nam-myoho-renge-kyo, they will all work to create value in relation to external circumstances.

Parts must be related to the whole in order to be of any use. If an arm is separated from the body, it cannot function. Only when an arm is part of the body can it fulfill the specific functions of writing, painting or holding things. When one's life is based on the Mystic Law, the ultimate truth of life, all one's activities will produce value. This will be achieved by performing gongyo daily. It ties the life-activities of the nine worlds directly to the Mystic Law, and thus charges them with the energy of Buddhahood.

As mentioned above, Shakyamuni's teachings contained in the Lotus Sutra are the "means" and the "truth" is Nam-myoho-renge-kyo. And from one viewpoint, even the practice Nichiren Daishonin revealed and taught is a means leading to the "end" of attaining Buddhahood. However, from a deeper viewpoint, carrying out this means in itself contains the end. Reciting a part of the Lotus Sutra and chanting daimoku is a means, while manifesting Buddhahood is the end. However, one manifests Buddhahood through the very act of reciting the Lotus Sutra and daimoku; means and end are thus inseparable.

The *Juryō* chapter reveals the unfathomable depth and duration of Shakyamuni's enlightenment. Hence the title: *ju* means the Buddha's life span, specifically that of Shakyamuni, and *ryō* means "to fathom." To "fathom the Buddha's life span" means to know how long he has been the Buddha. It does not mean that the *Juryō* chapter reveals the "eternity of life" itself. Belief in the eternity of life was widespread among virtually all ancient Indian philosophers long before the advent of Buddhism and therefore did not merit discussion in the *Juryō* chapter. The chapter focuses on the length of Shakyamuni's life as a Buddha, i.e., how much time has passed since he originally attained Buddhahood.

Here Shakyamuni introduces an unimaginably distant time called *gohyaku-jintengō,* when he first attained Buddhahood, and declares that since that time he has continually been here in this world preaching the Law in order to save humankind. His contemporaries looked upon Shakyamuni as a prince who began religious austerities as a youth and was finally enlightened near the town of Gayā. No one even considered the possibility that he might have been a Buddha before then, and when he did attain Buddhahood, they thought it was because he was someone special. The *Juryō* chapter showed the error of their views.

Still people were dubious. They wondered why the

Buddha, having attained enlightenment so long ago, was born a common mortal who carried out religious practices just as others do who are still seeking the way. Why was he not born a Buddha, they wondered. The answer to this question is that even when one has attained Buddhahood, the other nine worlds do not disappear from one's life. A Buddha appears in the world as an ordinary person possessing the nine worlds. This corresponds to the principle revealed in the *Hōben* chapter, that common mortals of the nine worlds all inherently possess the realm of Buddha. Buddhahood cannot exist apart from the nine worlds, nor vice versa, for both are forever inherent in life. This relationship is described as *himyō hōben*.

Although they both teach the inseparability of Buddhahood and the nine worlds, the *Hōben* and *Juryō* chapters are written from different viewpoints. That is, the *Hōben* chapter reveals that the nine worlds inherently possess Buddhahood, while the *Juryō* chapter shows that Buddhahood retains the nine worlds. In addition, the *Hōben* chapter shows Buddhahood only as a potential within people's lives, but the *Juryō* chapter depicts Buddhahood as a manifest reality in the person of Shakyamuni.

3. Three Expedients

SHAKYAMUNI Buddha gave many provisional teachings to his disciples as a means to lead them to the Lotus Sutra, his true teaching. All of the means he used are broadly divided into three categories according to their characteristics. The first group (*hōyū hōben*) consists of teachings which the Buddha expounded according to his disciples' inborn capacity or propensity. These correspond to Hinayana and early Mahayana teachings. What characterizes these teachings is that they all point to the impermanence of all phenomena and emphasize that by severing one's attachment to the affairs of this world one can acquire lasting happiness. This idea was acceptable to his disciples because they wished to emancipate themselves from earthly desires, and these teachings had them aim at personal salvation.

In the second group of teachings (*nōtsū hōben*) Shakyamuni denied the ideals his disciples had been seeking. He reproached them for being indifferent to the sufferings of others and striving only for their own salvation. Warning them, he stated that as long as they persisted in such selfish thinking, they would never attain Buddhahood. This second group of teachings belongs to a higher level of Mahayana Buddhism, but the teachings are still based on the premise that all phenomena are transitory.

The third category (*himyō hōben*) was used in the Lotus Sutra. Shakyamuni expounded the Lotus Sutra to transmit the truth which he had realized. The first two types of teachings constitute the provisional teachings and do not explain the truth in its entirety; they merely enhance the disciples' capability to understand it. Unlike these two expedients, *himyō hōben* is the teaching that not only leads people to the truth but simultaneously contains the truth. The word *hōben* (expedient means), which is the title of the second chapter of the Lotus Sutra, is this *himyō hōben*. *Himyō* means "concealed and unfathomable truth," implying that the truth is understood only by Buddhas.

The Lotus Sutra teaches that although all phenomena in the universe are impermanent, the ultimate reality permeating everything is eternally constant. Furthermore, it teaches that the ultimate reality is not separated from individual phenomena but manifests itself in phenomena. This principle is taught in the *Hōben* chapter of the Lotus Sutra. It tells us that Buddhas do not differ fundamentally from common mortals in the nine worlds (from Hell to Bodhisattva); they are essentially common mortals themselves. The difference between Buddhas and common mortals lies in whether they are enlightened to the truth that their lives and all phenomena in society are manifestations of the ultimate reality. Since ordinary wisdom cannot reach the truth that the Buddha realized, the truth remains "concealed" from common mortals, and therefore they have no recourse but to believe in the Buddha's teachings in order to attain the same enlightenment.

In Nichiren Daishonin's Buddhism, "benefit" and "punishment" or gain and loss are the expedient means (*himyō hōben*) which leads people to enlightenment.

4. Supreme Goal of Life

THE goals of Buddhist practice differ according to the teachings expounded by Shakyamuni. Earlier sutras set forth three provisional goals which remained paramount until the preaching of the Lotus Sutra. Thereafter, those provisional goals were permanently superseded by the supreme goal, which refers to the concept of "the replacement of the three vehicles with the one vehicle." The three vehicles are known as Learning, Realization and Bodhisattva; the one vehicle is Buddhahood. Through the Hinayana teachings, Shakyamuni's disciples were first led to seek the two vehicles of Learning and Realization. Believers who had achieved those states thought they could enter nirvana by eradicating all desires—including the desire to live. They believed that nirvana was a condition of voidness, without mind or body, in which the endless series of births and deaths and the suffering of this world would cease forever. But because they sought salvation for themselves without a thought for anyone else, Shakyamuni severely reprimanded them.

By contrast, in the greater part of the Mahayana teachings, Shakyamuni encouraged his disciples to become bodhisattvas and to postpone their entry into nirvana—although they could have entered at any moment—so that they could help others. The expansive Mahayana spirit is often contrasted with the narrow vision of Hinayana.

Despite the sharp contrast between the Hinayana and provisional Mahayana teachings they share one

major feature: both regard the Buddha as an enlightened one who stands far above a common mortal's
understanding. Buddhahood was believed to be something which one could attain only after practicing austerities over many lifetimes. When the Lotus Sutra was
expounded, however, Shakyamuni's disciples were all
fully awakened to the truth of life. They realized that
the Buddha nature, and the Buddha wisdom as well,
exist equally within all people. They understood that
they were capable of attaining Buddhahood just as their
mentor had. Shakyamuni clearly proclaimed that the
sole purpose of his advent in this world lay in helping all
people realize their innate Buddha nature and attain
Buddhahood. He went further by stating that they did
not require many lifetimes of practice to do so but that
they could become Buddhas themselves in their present form. All they had to do, Shakyamuni said, was to
believe in and live by the Mystic Law indicated in the
Lotus Sutra. Thus, the Lotus Sutra is the fount of self-
reformation, or human revolution, within the harsh
realities of society.

Since, therefore, Shakyamuni replaced the three vehicles with the "supreme vehicle" as the goal of Buddhist practice, are not the former now irrelevant? Most
certainly the goal of Buddhist faith and practice is to
attain Buddhahood, the supreme vehicle. However,
from the point of view of the Buddhist life philosophy,
the vehicles of Learning, Realization and Bodhisattva
are all indispensable aspects of life, because they are not
ends in themselves but a means to lead human beings
to the one Buddha vehicle. Moreover, in the propagation of Buddhism the three vehicles provide a way to

achieve the ability to pass on the true teaching to others. In this sense, the vehicle of Learning enables one to study the Buddhist doctrines, the vehicle of Realization leads one to an understanding that Buddhism really works in one's daily existence, and the vehicle of Bodhisattva leads one to feel sympathy and act in a compassionate manner toward unhappy people.

5. Enlightenment of the Two Vehicles

In the Lotus Sutra, those of the two vehicles, voice-hearers and cause-awakened ones, including Shāriputra and Mahākāshyapa, receive a prophecy from Shakyamuni Buddha that they will attain Buddhahood sometime in the future. This prophecy stands in striking contrast to the teachings of all the other sutras, which denounce those persons of the two vehicles for seeking only personal salvation and assert that the seed of Buddhahood can never be manifest in their egotistic minds, as though the seed had been scorched and destroyed.

The Lotus Sutra proclaims that Shakyamuni's disciples of the two vehicles were able to receive a specific prophecy of their eventual attainment of Buddhahood when they listened to the teachings revealed in the sutra and vowed to strive to save suffering people. They are divided into the three groups of superior, intermediate and lesser capacity, according to how readily they grasped the Buddha's teaching. Shāriputra alone understood immediately upon hearing the Buddha preach concerning "the true entity of all phenomena" in the

Hōben (second) chapter; he comprises the first group. His enlightenment is predicted in the *Hiyu* (third) chapter. Mahākāshyapa, Kātyāyana, Subhūti and Maudgalyāyana understood the Buddha's teaching through the parable of the three carts and the burning house* related in the *Hiyu* chapter. They represent the second group, whose attainment of Buddhahood is predicted in the *Juki* (sixth) chapter. The other twelve hundred disciples finally understood the Buddha's teaching by hearing about their relationship with Shakyamuni since the remote past of *sanzen-jintengō*, as explained in the *Kejōyu* (seventh) chapter.† They constitute the third group. They were also assured of future enlightenment in the next chapter.

The sutras expounded before the Lotus Sutra asserted that the voice-hearers and the cause-awakened ones were eternally incapable of attaining Buddhahood. The Lotus Sutra revealed that even those of the two vehicles can become Buddhas. Therefore, it verifies that all people are able to attain Buddhahood without any exception. In the pre-Lotus Sutra teachings, those who aspired toward enlightenment were required to carry out the practice of the six *pāramitās* over a period of countless kalpas. Thus, enlightenment was entirely impossible for ordinary people. Voice-hearers thought that those pre-Lotus Sutra teachings were unable to

*This parable illustrates the sole purpose of the Buddha's advent—all people's attainment of Buddhahood. The three carts—pulled by a sheep, a deer and an ox—represent the three provisional vehicles of Learning, Realization and Bodhisattva, and the burning house represents this troubled world. The Buddha appears in this world in order to lead the people to the supreme vehicle of Buddhahood.

†See p. 116.

save the people, and as a result, they sought only their personal enlightenment. In contrast, the Lotus Sutra declared that all people inherently possess the Buddha nature within their lives and thus clarified the way for anyone to attain Buddhahood in this lifetime. The way is to awaken to the presence of the Buddha nature, that is, to believe in the teaching of the Buddha who realized it. Consequently, it was not until the persons of the two vehicles heard the Buddha expound the Lotus Sutra that they realized it is possible to save and lead all people to enlightenment. Finally they were able to liberate themselves from the confines of egoism.

6. Why the Buddha Appears

THE *Hōben* (second) chapter of the Lotus Sutra states that all Buddhas appear in the world solely in order to "open the door of Buddha wisdom to all beings, show it, cause them to awaken to it and induce them to enter into it." That is, the purpose of a Buddha's appearance in the world is to awaken in all people the Buddha wisdom, help them realize it and enable them to attain Buddhahood. "Buddha wisdom" signifies the wisdom that Buddhas alone possess. This is equal to "the wisdom of all Buddhas" which appears at the beginning of the same chapter. "The wisdom of all Buddhas" is the wisdom which Buddhas, without exception, possess in common. This "wisdom" is the essential quality of the Buddha. At the same time this wisdom leads all

Buddhas to their realization of the ultimate truth. Only in the Latter Day of the Law did Nichiren Daishonin clarify the Buddha wisdom, the ultimate truth, as Nam-myoho-renge-kyo. Four acts—opening, showing, awakening and entering—comprise the process undertaken by all people of the nine worlds to manifest the Buddha wisdom inherent in their lives and to attain Buddhahood.

In the "Ongi kuden" (Record of the Orally Transmitted Teachings) Nichiren Daishonin says that "to open" is "to believe." That is, "to open" means to believe firmly in the Buddha wisdom, or potential Buddhahood, inherent in one's life. With firm faith that the Buddha's infinite wisdom exists within, there is always hope for the future. "To show" thus means to manifest that hope. With hope and belief in the boundless power and wisdom inherent in life, this wisdom is available to overcome the problems and difficulties of daily existence and of society. This means "to awaken" through one's own experiences to the power of wisdom to overcome difficulties. "To enter" means to enter the state of absolute freedom and happiness, or to attain a state of perfection. However, absolute freedom does not mean to transcend one's physical limitations and external influences completely. It is a state of perfection attained in the innermost realm of life.

7. Treasure Tower, the Two Buddhas

THE *Hōtō* (eleventh) chapter of the Lotus Sutra describes the appearance of an imposing and magnificent-
ly bejeweled tower. It states that the tower measures
500 *yojana* high, 250 *yojana* wide and 250 *yojana* deep.
According to one interpretation, 500 *yojana* would be
equal to the radius of the earth. Since the tower was
adorned with seven kinds of gems, including gold and
silver, it was called Treasure Tower. It also has been
called the Tower of Tahō, for it was in this tower that
Tahō Buddha was seated. The name "Tahō" literally
means many treasures.

The purpose of Tahō's appearance was to validate the
truth of the teaching expounded in the former part of
the Lotus Sutra. From within the Treasure Tower he
proclaimed: "All that you [Shakyamuni] have expounded is the truth." Tahō Buddha himself did not expound
or preach any teachings; his only purpose was to attest
to the validity of Shakyamuni's teaching. Consequently,
the two Buddhas, Tahō and Shakyamuni, represent
objective verification or actual proof and subjective
wisdom or enlightenment, respectively.

It was not only Tahō Buddha who fulfilled the role of
proving the Buddha's teachings. The Treasure Tower
itself also fulfilled this purpose. The first ten chapters of
the Lotus Sutra state that Shakyamuni's disciples such as
Shāriputra and Mahākāshyapa would become enlightened to the Buddha nature inherent within the depths
of their lives through Shakyamuni's teaching and be

able to attain Buddhahood. The Treasure Tower symbolizes the grandeur and dignity of this innate Buddha nature as well as a shift from a theoretical perception to the actual manifestation of the Buddha nature. The jewels which adorn the Treasure Tower signify power, wisdom, fortune and the other positive characteristics of an enlightened life.

Shakyamuni then opened the Treasure Tower and at Tahō's invitation seated himself at this Buddha's side. Shakyamuni and Tahō seated side by side in the Treasure Tower signifies the fusion of reality and wisdom (*kyōchi myōgō*). Shakyamuni represents the Buddha's enlightened wisdom inherent in all people, in particular in those of the two vehicles (voice-hearers and cause-awakened ones) who attended the ceremony of the Lotus Sutra, and Tahō, the objective and unchanging truth that all people inherently possess the Buddha nature. In order to realize this truth one has to activate one's innate wisdom, after which the fusion of wisdom and truth leads one to the attainment of Buddhahood.

Nichiren Daishonin embodied the ceremony of the Treasure Tower described in the Lotus Sutra into the Gohonzon. Therefore, in concrete terms, the Treasure Tower is the Gohonzon and, in a broad sense, the life of those who manifest their inherent Buddhahood by chanting Nam-myoho-renge-kyo.

8. Reality and Wisdom

THE unity of subject and object, *kyōchi myōgō,* is a very important concept in the understanding of Buddhism. *Kyō* indicates the objective reality or truth of the Buddha nature inherent within one's life, and *chi* means the subjective wisdom to realize that truth. In the Lotus Sutra, Tahō Buddha, seated in the Treasure Tower, represents objective reality. Then, at Tahō's invitation, Shakyamuni seats himself beside this Buddha. Shakyamuni represents subjective wisdom. That they sat together within the tower signifies the fusion of reality and wisdom. From the viewpoint of life philosophy, Tahō Buddha is the Buddha nature inherent in one's life. Shakyamuni Buddha represents the wisdom to realize the Buddha nature. Merely to possess the Buddha nature does not, however, mean that one is actually a Buddha. When one awakens to the existence of the Buddha nature within, in other words, when one's subjective wisdom is completely fused with the objective reality or the truth, then the Buddha nature actually manifests itself from within the depths of one's life. Accordingly, the fusion of wisdom and reality is itself the attainment of Buddhahood.

Nichiren Daishonin embodied his enlightenment—the fusion of reality and wisdom—in the form of the Gohonzon, the object of worship. The Gohonzon itself is the entity of the fusion of reality and wisdom, for Shakyamuni and Tahō are positioned in it, representing Buddhahood. In terms of Buddhist practice for people in the Latter Day of the Law, when they chant Nam-myoho-renge-kyo with deep faith in the Gohonzon, the fusion of reality and wisdom will take place within their own lives, so that they will be able to realize the Buddha nature and attain Buddhahood. Thus faith equals wisdom. Again, the Buddha nature is reality and faith in the Gohonzon corresponds to wisdom. Hence Nichiren Daishonin says in his Gosho "The Real Aspect of the Gohonzon," "Never seek this Gohonzon outside yourself. The Gohonzon exists only within the mortal flesh of us ordinary people who embrace the Lotus Sutra and chant Nam-myoho-renge-kyo."*

In the ceremony of the Lotus Sutra, Tahō Buddha, Shakyamuni Buddha and the Buddhas from throughout the universe represent the three bodies of a single Buddha. Tahō indicates the Dharma body, or the property of the Law, Shakyamuni, the bliss body, or the property of wisdom, and all the other Buddhas, the manifested body, or the property of action. The gathering of all these Buddhas at the ceremony of the Lotus Sutra signifies that this entire ceremony represents the original Buddha eternally endowed with the three bodies, that is, the Buddha of Nam-myoho-renge-kyo.

9. Ceremony in the Air

In the *Hōtō* (eleventh) chapter of the Lotus Sutra, the Treasure Tower emerges from the earth and remains suspended in midair. Shakyamuni Buddha joins Tahō Buddha, seated side by side in it. This begins the Cere-

*Major Writings, vol. 1, p. 213.

mony in the Air. Shakyamuni then reveals his original enlightenment in the remote past of *gohyaku-jintengō* and transfers the essence of the sutra to the Bodhisattvas of the Earth led by Bodhisattva Jōgyō, entrusting them with its propagation after his passing. In the *Zokurui* (twenty-second) chapter, he transfers the sutra to all the bodhisattvas. Then all the Buddhas who assembled from throughout the universe return to their own lands, and the Treasure Tower reverts to its original state; the Ceremony in the Air comes to an end.

According to the Indian customs of the time, kings and high dignitaries seated themselves facing east. It is conceivable, therefore, that early in his preaching of the Lotus Sutra on Eagle Peak, Shakyamuni Buddha looked eastward and his disciples faced him in the west. Later, the Treasure Tower appeared, facing toward the west in the presence of Shakyamuni and the audience, and floated into space. Shakyamuni ascended into the air and seated himself beside Tahō, who was inside the tower. Therefore, Shakyamuni faced west when he expounded the Lotus Sutra during the Ceremony in the Air. The entire assembly, lifted into space by Shakyamuni's supernatural powers, attended the ceremony, facing the tower in the east.

In the *Kanji* (thirteenth) chapter, at the urging of Shakyamuni Buddha, Bodhisattva Yakuō and eight hundred thousand million nayutas (a nayuta is equivalent to 10^{11}) of bodhisattvas make a vow to propagate the Lotus Sutra after his death. The innumerable bodhisattvas who have assembled from other worlds then vow to spread the sutra in this world after Shakyamuni's passing, as depicted at the beginning of the *Yujutsu* (fifteenth) chapter. Shakyamuni stops them, however, and instead calls forth a host of great bodhisattvas, equal in number to the sands of sixty thousand Ganges rivers, from below the earth. He says that these bodhisattvas are his original disciples. Bodhisattva Miroku, astounded at this sight, asks the Buddha on behalf of the assembly how he has managed to teach so many countless bodhisattvas. To answer his question, Shakyamuni reveals in the *Juryō* (sixteenth) chapter that he attained Buddhahood in the remote past of *gohyaku-jintengō* and that he has been training these Bodhisattvas of the Earth since then. In the *Jinriki* (twenty-first) chapter, he transfers the essence of the sutra specifically to the Bodhisattvas of the Earth, and in the *Zokurui* chapter, he transfers the sutra to all the assembled bodhisattvas in general.

What does the Ceremony in the Air symbolize? What does Shakyamuni attempt to impart through this ceremony? In reply, it is necessary to consider what would happen if the ceremony had been held at Eagle Peak. In that case, the ceremony would inevitably have been bound by geographical or spatial and historical or temporal limitations, for Eagle Peak (Skt Gridhrakūta) is a mountain located in India and Shakyamuni lived some three thousand years ago. In contrast, the ceremony held in the air implies a transcendence of the confines of time and space. It also suggests that what was expressed during this ceremony is the eternal and universal truth which transcends the framework of time and space. Nichiren Daishonin states that the

Gohonzon is the perfect embodiment of his own enlightenment, and that what is depicted on the Gohonzon and in the Ceremony in the Air is essentially the
same.

10. Enlightenment of Devadatta and the Dragon King's Daughter

THE *Devadatta* (twelfth) chapter of the Lotus Sutra
teaches that both Devadatta and the dragon king's
daughter are capable of attaining Buddhahood. This
chapter is not a separate chapter in the extant Sanskrit
original; it is said to have been made one of the twenty-
eight chapters of the Lotus Sutra in later ages. In terms
of content, however, in the *Hōtō* (eleventh) chapter
Shakyamuni stresses the necessity of the Lotus Sutra's
propagation after his passing, and in the *Devadatta* chapter he declares that the sutra is the only teaching which
is able to save all people in an evil-ridden age that will
come some two thousand years after his death.

In the first half of the *Devadatta* chapter, Shakyamuni
Buddha discloses that countless kalpas ago he was a king
who renounced his throne in order to seek the truth.
For one thousand years he served a hermit named Ashi,
withstanding all ordeals, and the hermit in return
taught him the Lotus Sutra. This hermit, he explains, is
none other than the present Devadatta. Devadatta in
his present life had tried on several occasions to kill the
Buddha and to destroy the unity of the Buddhist order,
and is said to have fallen into hell alive. However,

Shakyamuni prophesies that in the distant future Devadatta will attain enlightenment as a Buddha called
Heavenly King.

The *Devadatta* chapter also describes the enlightenment of the dragon king's daughter. Bodhisattva Monju
relates that, when he preached the Lotus Sutra in the
palace of the dragon king, an eight-year-old daughter of
the king displayed a profound understanding of the
sutra. Bodhisattva Chishaku and Shāriputra both challenge this, on the grounds that women are said to be incapable of attaining enlightenment. By now the dragon
girl has appeared in front of them. After presenting
a jewel to Shakyamuni Buddha, she at once manifests
her attainment of Buddhahood in her dragon form.

The attainment of Buddhahood by Devadatta and
the dragon king's daughter has several implications.
First, in terms of the Ten Worlds, Devadatta represents
the state of Hell, and the dragon king's daughter represents a being of the world of Animality. In short, it symbolizes the possibility of enlightenment for even those
in the worlds of Hell and Animality. Furthermore, the
fact that evil people, personified by Devadatta, and stu-
pid people, represented by the dragon king's daughter,
can attain enlightenment illustrates the universal possibility of Buddhahood which the Lotus Sutra teaches. In
the final analysis, their attainment of Buddhahood
reveals that the power and benefit of the Lotus Sutra
enable all people equally to gain enlightenment, and
through the practice of the Mystic Law indicated in the
sutra even those people of the Latter Day of the Law,
whose lives are polluted and distorted, can reach the
supreme state of Buddhahood.

11. Three Powerful Enemies

IN the *Kanji* (thirteenth) chapter of the Lotus Sutra, the numerous bodhisattvas swore to propagate Buddhism in the turbulent age after the death of Shakyamuni Buddha. According to this sutra, this age will be filled with strife and conflict, and suffering will befall them. They nonetheless volunteered to spread Buddhism and vowed to stand up to any kind of hardship. The three powerful enemies were said to be the most difficult of the trials lying in wait for them. Having made this vow, these bodhisattvas were stunned when Shakyamuni rejected their offer and instead called forth the Bodhisattvas of the Earth, entrusting them alone with the mission of propagating the Mystic Law in the future evil age.

No Bodhisattva of the Earth can spread the Mystic Law without meeting the three powerful enemies. These were defined by Miao-lo of China in his *Hokke mongu ki* (Annotations on the *Words and Phrases of the Lotus Sutra*) on the basis of descriptions in the *Kanji* chapter. They are characterized as: (1) lay people ignorant of Buddhism who denounce the votaries of the Lotus Sutra and attack them with swords and staves; (2) arrogant and cunning priests who, although still having much to learn about Buddhism, boast that they have attained the highest truth and who slander the votaries; and (3) priests revered as saints and respected by the general public who, in fear of losing fame or profit, induce the secular authorities to persecute the votaries of the Lotus Sutra.

In practical terms, the first enemy refers to ordinary people who have little knowledge of Buddhism, and the second to learned priests who are believed to be well versed in Buddhism. The third enemy indicates those who, having authority in the religious world as well as a fair knowledge of Buddhism, join with those of authority in society at large and instigate them to oppress believers. The third is the strongest and greatest of all enemies.

Nichiren Daishonin personally experienced all of the persecutions indicated in the *Kanji* chapter and fulfilled his mission, never once yielding to any of them. In this sense, too, he "lived" the Lotus Sutra exactly as it teaches. In meeting the three powerful enemies, he was able to confirm that he himself was the leader of the Bodhisattvas of the Earth.

12. Bodhisattvas of the Earth

THE *Yujutsu* (fifteenth) chapter of the Lotus Sutra describes the appearance of innumerable bodhisattvas from beneath the earth. Thus they are called, quite literally, Bodhisattvas of the Earth.

Shakyamuni Buddha earlier expressed his desire to entrust the Law to those courageous enough to propagate the Lotus Sutra after his death, during the future Latter Day of the Law. He emphasized the difficulty of propagating the sutra in the Latter Day and described the occurrence of various obstacles such as the three powerful enemies.

In the *Yujutsu* chapter, a multitude of bodhisattvas emerged from beneath the earth, each with his own retinue of followers. They were led by the four bodhisattvas—Jōgyō (Superior Conduct), Muhengyō (Limitless Conduct), Jyōgyō (Pure Conduct) and Anryūgyō (Conduct of Standing Firm)—and Jōgyō was the leader of them all. Later on in the sutra, Shakyamuni transferred the essence of the Lotus Sutra to these Bodhisattvas of the Earth, entrusting them with the mission of propagating it in the Latter Day. Those who now devote themselves to propagating the Mystic Law are none other than the Bodhisattvas of the Earth.

The "earth" from which the bodhisattvas came means Nam-myoho-renge-kyo, or the life of the cosmos itself. It is the Buddha nature inherent in all things—living and nonliving—throughout the universe. The Bodhisattvas of the Earth make Nam-myoho-renge-kyo the basis of their being and originally dwell in the "earth" of Buddhahood, or Nam-myoho-renge-kyo. Drawing on the infinite power of Buddhahood, they propagate the Mystic Law throughout the world and relieve the people from their suffering. The Bodhisattvas of the Earth chose to appear in this trouble-ridden world. In other words, they are functions of the Buddha nature of *kuon ganjo,* time without beginning, and the Buddha nature is their basic essence. Its power manifests itself in the activities of these bodhisattvas.

Nichiren Daishonin is the original Buddha of *kuon ganjo,* but during the ceremony when the Lotus Sutra was expounded, he appeared in the form of Bodhisattva Jōgyō, the leader of the Bodhisattvas of the Earth.

Before the Tatsunokuchi Persecution in 1271, Nichiren Daishonin devoted his entire being to the mission of propagating the essence of the Lotus Sutra or Nam-myoho-renge-kyo, thereby identifying himself as Bodhisattva Jōgyō. After this incident, however, he emerged from his transient status as Bodhisattva Jōgyō and revealed his true identity as the original Buddha who made his advent in the Latter Day of the Law.

In the capacity of the original Buddha, the Daishonin not only bestowed on humankind a wealth of teachings but also embodied his enlightenment in the Gohonzon as the object of worship to enable all people to attain Buddhahood. Thus, Nichiren Daishonin dedicated his entire life to the perpetuation of the Mystic Law throughout the Latter Day.

13. Bodhisattvas Taught by a Provisional Buddha

WHAT is the difference between the Bodhisattvas of the Earth and other bodhisattvas, such as Monju and Yakuō? One way to illustrate the difference is to study the relationship between a true Buddha and a provisional Buddha. The former is like a material object and the latter, its shadow. As the object moves, its shadow moves. Even when the object remains still, if the light casting the shadow changes position, the shadow will change position as well. Thus, the same object can project different shadows under different conditions. Likewise, the Buddha has many different aspects according to the age in which he appears. Sometimes he reveals only several of these, but at other times he reveals himself completely. In the former case he is called a provisional Buddha, and in the latter case he is known as the true Buddha.

The Bodhisattvas of the Earth are followers of a true Buddha, or the Buddha who revealed his true identity. (The Buddha in this status is called the true Buddha.) In the essential teaching of the Lotus Sutra, Shakyamuni revealed his true identity as the Buddha who first attained enlightenment in the remote past. The disciples whom he taught in this capacity are known as the bodhisattvas taught by the true Buddha, that is, the Bodhisattvas of the Earth who appear in the *Yujutsu* (fifteenth) chapter. Shakyamuni Buddha expounded his original enlightenment and entrusted them with the mission of propagating the essence of the sutra in the Latter Day of the Law. Therefore, the Bodhisattvas of the Earth are able to teach and spread the Mystic Law directly. On the other hand, there are the bodhisattvas taught by a Buddha in his transient status. In the pre-Lotus Sutra teachings and in the theoretical teaching of the Lotus Sutra, Shakyamuni assumed the provisional status of the Buddha who had first attained enlightenment in that lifetime. (The Buddha in this status is called a provisional Buddha.) The bodhisattvas he taught in this capacity, such as Monju, perceived only part of the Buddha's enlightenment. Figuratively, they were given only the shadow of the Buddha and could therefore expound Buddhism only partially.

From the viewpoint of the ten states of life, to be a bodhisattva is to be in a state of life filled with compassion and the wish to save other people from suffering. However, the methods of the two kinds of bodhisattvas differ. The Bodhisattvas of the Earth help people by leading them to believe in the ultimate Law of Nammyoho-renge-kyo, or the Buddha's original enlightenment. The other bodhisattvas try to help people by inspiring them with wisdom, courage and other virtues. For example, Bodhisattva Monju represents wisdom, Bodhisattva Miroku signifies compassion, Bodhisattva Kannon indicates the correct assessment of the prevailing social circumstances, and Bodhisattva Fugen implies the power of knowledge. In contrast with the Bodhisattvas of the Earth, who serve to draw strong life force directly from the Mystic Law inherent in human life and in the cosmos, these bodhisattvas use their specific skills to benefit society.

14. Shakyamuni's Enlightenment

THE true goal of Buddhist faith and practice is revealed in the first half of the Lotus Sutra. In the latter half another important truth is expounded. It is called "opening the near and revealing the distant." "Opening the near" means Shakyamuni's refutation of the view that he, born as Gautama Siddhārtha, practiced various austerities and attained enlightenment for the first time at Buddhagayā. In the *Juryō* (sixteenth) chapter of the Lotus Sutra, Shakyamuni disclosed that he had attained Buddhahood in the distant past of *gohyaku-jintengō*.

Gohyaku-jintengō indicates how immeasurably long

ago Shakyamuni attained enlightenment for the first time, and it is considered a concept similar to the eternity of life. The eternity of life was a widely known concept developed in Brahmanism, before the emergence of Buddhism, and the idea of transmigration, in which life never actually is extinguished, was also generally accepted among the people in ancient India, and can be found among the concepts of Pythagoras and other Greek philosophers. Even in scriptures prior to the Lotus Sutra it is stated that Shakyamuni had practiced bodhisattva austerities in many past existences. However, the *Juryō* chapter reveals that the enlightened life of Shakyamuni as the Buddha which was manifested in his lifetime, when he was born as Gautama Siddhārtha, had continued uninterrupted from the extremely remote period known as *gohyaku-jintengō*. People wondered, "If that were the case, why did Shakyamuni, who had been enlightened for such a long time, appear as a common mortal and practice austerities under Brahman teachers?" Both the question and the answer given in the Lotus Sutra demanded a change in popular preconceptions about the Buddha. According to the provisional Mahayana teachings expounded before the Lotus Sutra, to attain Buddhahood meant to end the sufferings caused by transmigration. When a person attained Buddhahood, it was thought that he was no longer required to be born into this world. However, the *Juryō* chapter explains that even if one attains enlightenment, the nine worlds (from Hell to Bodhisattva) within one's life will never disappear but will exist eternally. The nine worlds take on a new meaning in that they are shown to be controlled by the

Buddha nature working within one's life. This is the principle that the nine worlds all exist within the state of Buddhahood, and conversely, as stated in the *Hōben* (second) chapter of the Lotus Sutra, that Buddhahood is inherent within the nine worlds. Yet even more important is the question of the Law to which Shakyamuni became enlightened for the first time at *gohyaku-jintengō*. With this, the way was opened to Nichiren Daishonin's Buddhism.

15. True and Provisional Buddhas

THE true identity of the Buddha and the temporary aspects he assumes can be compared, respectively, to the moon shining in the sky and its reflection on the surface of a pond. The former is called the true Buddha, and the latter are called provisional Buddhas. The teachings expounded by the true Buddha are called essential teaching and those left by a provisional Buddha, theoretical teaching. It was the Great Teacher T'ien-t'ai of China who established the two ideas of "true" and "provisional," comparing them to the moon and its reflection on the water.

In the theoretical teaching (first half) of the Lotus Sutra, as well as in the sutras taught before it, Shakyamuni stated that he attained enlightenment in India for the first time at the age of thirty. However, in the essential teaching (latter half) of the Lotus Sutra, he denied the former statement and revealed that he first attained enlightenment in the distant past of *gohyaku-jintengō*. As long as Shakyamuni said that he realized Buddhahood in India, he was a provisional Buddha, but when he revealed his original enlightenment in *gohyaku-jintengō,* he was acting as the true Buddha who disclosed his true identity. Bodhisattvas such as Monju and Miroku are the disciples of the provisional Buddha, and the Bodhisattvas of the Earth are the disciples of the true Buddha.

In the sutras expounded before the Lotus Sutra, Shakyamuni said that in past existences he practiced Buddhist austerities by appearing as many different persons such as Sessen Dōji* and King Shibi.† All these figures are, so to speak, provisional aspects of Shakyamuni's true identity.

Nichiren Daishonin identified himself as the original Buddha who had been enlightened to the ultimate truth since the infinite past, far older than even the inconceivably distant past of *gohyaku-jintengō.* Moreover, he clarified the original cause for Shakyamuni's enlightenment as the ultimate Law of Nam-myoho-renge-kyo. Therefore, the theory of Shakyamuni's enlightenment at *gohyaku-jintengō* still does not explain

*Sessen Dōji: According to the Nirvana Sutra, when Sessen Dōji was practicing austerities in the Snow Mountains, the god Taishaku appeared in the form of a demon and recited half a verse from a Buddhist teaching. Sessen Dōji begged the demon to tell him the second half. The demon demanded his flesh and blood in payment. Sessen Dōji consented, and the demon taught him the latter half of the verse. He scrawled this teaching on the rocks and trees, and then jumped from a tall tree. Just at that moment the demon changed back into Taishaku and caught him.

†Shibi: The name of Shakyamuni when he was a king carrying out the practice of almsgiving. One day the god Bishukatsuma disguised himself as a dove and Taishaku changed into a hawk in order to test King Shibi. The hawk relentlessly pursued the dove, which flew into Shibi's robes for protection. In order to save the dove, Shibi offered his flesh to the starving hawk.

the Buddha's true entity in its entirety, which is why, from the standpoint of the Daishonin's Buddhism, even Shakyamuni is called a provisional Buddha, and Nichiren Daishonin, the manifestation of the original Buddha from time without beginning, is called the true Buddha who appeared as the Buddha of the Latter Day of the Law.

In order to project an image, in the same way that the moon is reflected on the surface of a pond, a screen is necessary. Nichiren Daishonin is also the reincarnation of Bodhisattva Jōgyō, who can be thought of as an image projected by the original Buddha onto the screen of the Lotus Sutra. Even Shakyamuni was but an image of the original Buddha when he expounded the essential teaching, inasmuch as he was only able to reveal a part of his true eternal entity.

Human beings are, in the innermost depths of their lives, the original entities of the Mystic Law. Born as human beings on this planet, people dedicate themselves, in their role of the Bodhisattvas of the Earth, to the spread of the Mystic Law throughout the world. They project various images onto the "screen" of society, as a husband or wife in the home; a clerk, secretary or scholar at work; a teacher or student at school, and so forth. The roles they carry out are continually changing, yet the true entity of life, or the Buddha nature inherent in each individual, is eternal and unchangeable.

16. *Sanzen-jintengō* and *Gohyaku-jintengō*

THE two periods of time, *sanzen-jintengō* and *gohyaku-jintengō*, are defined in the Lotus Sutra. The former is explained in the *Kejōyu* (seventh) chapter of the sutra to indicate how much time has passed since Shakyamuni Buddha preached the Lotus Sutra to his disciples such as Shāriputra and Mahākāshyapa. *Sanzen* of *sanzen-jintengō*, "three thousand," indicates a major world system (*sanzen-daisen-sekai*, consisting of $1,000^3$ worlds and corresponding to today's concept of one galaxy) that one originally reduces to dust in beginning its calculation. *Jinten* means placing all the dust particles side by side and *gō* means kalpa. In the *Kejōyu* chapter *sanzen-jintengō* is described as follows:

> If a person should use his strength to smash
> the ground of a major world system,
> should completely crush its earth particles
> and reduce them all to powdered ink,
> and if when he passed through a thousand lands
> he should drop one speck of ink,
> and if he continued in this manner
> until he had exhausted all the specks of ink,
> and if one then took the soil of the lands he had
>   passed through,
> both those he dropped a speck in and those he
>   did not,
> and once more ground their earth into dust,
> and then took one grain of dust to represent one
>   kalpa—

the number of tiny grains of dust would be less
than the number of kalpas in the past when that
Buddha lived.
Since that Buddha passed into extinction,
an immeasurable number of kalpas such as this
have passed.

"That Buddha" refers to Daitsūchishō (Great Universal Wisdom Excellence) Buddha, and "an immeasurable number of kalpas" refers to *sanzen-jintengō*. Shakyamuni declared that in the remote past of *sanzen-jintengō*
he was born as the last of the sixteen sons of Daitsūchishō Buddha, who was formerly a king. This Buddha expounded the Lotus Sutra, and his sons, blessed by
the chance to hear their father's teaching, transmitted it
to a great number of people. Those who were taught by
the Buddha's sixteenth son were later reborn in India
together with Shakyamuni in order to complete their
Buddhist practice for attaining enlightenment.

One important point to mention is that according to
the first half of the Lotus Sutra, called the theoretical
teaching, Shakyamuni had not yet attained Buddhahood as the son of Daitsūchishō Buddha in *sanzen-
jintengō*. He was said to have attained Buddhahood for
the first time when he appeared in India.

A much longer period called *gohyaku-jintengō* is described in the *Juryō* (sixteenth) chapter of the Lotus
Sutra. This chapter records Shakyamuni's disclosure
that he had actually attained Buddhahood an unimaginably long time before his advent in India—in a period known as *gohyaku-jintengō*. *Gohyaku*, literally "five
hundred," stands for the five hundred, a thousand, ten

thousand, a million, nayuta (10^{11}), asōgi (10^{59}) major world systems.

The chapter reads:

> Suppose a person were to take five hundred, a thousand, ten thousand, a million nayuta asōgi major world systems and grind them to dust. Then, moving eastward, each time he passes five hundred, a thousand, ten thousand, a million nayuta asōgi worlds he drops a particle of dust. He continues eastward in this way until he has finished dropping all the particles. . . . Suppose all these worlds, whether they received a particle of dust or not, are once more reduced to dust. Let one particle represent one kalpa. The time that has passed since I attained Buddhahood surpasses this by a hundred, a thousand, ten thousand, a million nayuta asōgi kalpas.

Therefore, the latter half of the Lotus Sutra, called the essential teaching, declares that Shakyamuni had already attained Buddhahood in *gohyaku-jintengō,* which preceded *sanzen-jintengō* by an incomparably long time. Clearly the teachings of these two chapters of the sutra are contradictory. Is it true that Shakyamuni educated his disciples in the remote past of *sanzen-jintengō,* not as a Buddha but as a prince? This is resolved only by reviewing the first half of the sutra from the standpoint of the latter. In spite of having attained Buddhahood in *gohyaku-jintengō,* Shakyamuni assumed a transient status by appearing as a prince in *sanzen-jintengō* in order to save the people of that age, because as a prince he had contact with great numbers of people.

As is stated in the *Juryō* chapter, Shakyamuni attained enlightenment for the first time in *gohyaku-jintengō*. But Nichiren Daishonin's teachings expound a far more distant period of time than *gohyaku-jintengō*. It is called *kuon ganjo*, which is defined as the beginningless infinite past. *Kuon ganjo* is eternal just like the universe, and Nichiren Daishonin is the original Buddha of *kuon ganjo*. However, he made his appearance in the Latter Day of the Law and propagated the Mystic Law, the essence of the Lotus Sutra, in his capacity as Bodhisattva Jōgyō. This is understandable in terms of the principle of the Buddha's transient status and his true identity.

17. Concept of Time—Kalpa

KALPA designates an extremely long period of time in the language of the ancient Indian tradition. There are various views on the length of a kalpa. According to one explanation, a kalpa is longer than the time required to wear away a huge cube of stone, if a heavenly nymph alights on it and brushes it with a piece of cloth once every one hundred years.

The most common way of conceptualizing a kalpa concerns the span of human life. Starting with a period in which the life span of a human being is an unimaginably long 80,000 years, reduce it a year every 100 years until it is only 10 years. Then, reversing the process, add one year to the life span every 100 years until it finally returns to 80,000. Then, calculating the time for the decrease from 80,000 to 10 years, 79,990 multiplied by

100 equals 7,999,000 years. As the same calculations are involved in increasing from 10 to 80,000, two times 7,999,000 equals 15,998,000 years. Thus, one kalpa is usually said to be 16 million minus 2,000 years.

The sutras say that twenty times one kalpa equals a medium kalpa, and one who commits the sin of killing a parent or wounding a Buddha is doomed to fall into the hell of incessant suffering and to stay there for one medium kalpa. In contrast, it is stated in the Lotus Sutra that those who persecuted Bodhisattva Fukyō—who was devoted to the propagation of the twenty-four-character teaching and who showed respect toward all people for their inherent Buddha nature—even though they repented in the end, had to stay in the hell of incessant suffering for one thousand kalpas. In fact, it specifies one thousand medium kalpas. That is why Nichiren Daishonin stated in the Gosho that the offense of slandering the true teachings of Buddhism and its believers is one thousand times graver than that of murder.

All phenomena in the universe undergo constant change—the perpetual cycle of formation (the birth and growth period), continuance (the stage in which growth stops and forms of life maintain themselves in full maturity), decline (the waning period) and disintegration (the stage in which phenomena merge with the universe after the collapse of the physical form). According to Buddhist cosmology, the universe perpetually repeats this four-stage cycle, and the periods of time corresponding to these four stages are called the four kalpas. The length of each of these four kalpas consists of a medium kalpa, and the time required for the entire process to elapse is called a major kalpa. That makes one major kalpa approximately 1,280 million years, using the above method of calculation, but it is only one way to estimate the length of a kalpa. The Buddhist view does not necessarily consider this to be the accurate way to determine the age of the universe.

Today there is no clear evidence as to which view concerning the length of a kalpa is most accurate. Although it is vague, the concept is found widely in Buddhism, together with numbers and epithets, as part of more complex calculations, such as *sanzen-jintengō* and *gohyaku-jintengō*. *Gō* in the last syllables of these two terms is a phonetic change of kalpa, or *kō* in Japanese.

18. One Chapter and Two Halves

THE "one chapter and two halves" is the core of the Lotus Sutra, comprising the latter half of the *Yujutsu* (fifteenth) chapter, the entire *Juryō* (sixteenth) chapter and the first half of the *Fumbetsu kudoku* (seventeenth) chapter. This section reveals Shakyamuni's original enlightenment in the remote past, and the fact that implicit in that revelation is the cause which enabled Shakyamuni to attain enlightenment in the inconceivably distant past of *gohyaku-jintengō*. The cause is indicative of the fundamental Law which leads all people to attain the same Buddhahood as Shakyamuni. They are able to attain enlightenment by being awakened to the Law.

Furthermore, the Buddha's life, which has always existed since his original enlightenment, represents

the Buddha nature or Buddhahood. Many different
Buddhas with their own functions of wisdom who
appeared in order to instruct particular people at specific times are merely provisional manifestations of
this eternal state of Buddhahood. The Buddha's life,
which has existed since the immemorial past, corresponds to the Buddha of absolute freedom (*jijuyūshin*),
who derives limitless joy from the Law and directly
expounds the Law which he has realized; however, the
Buddha of beneficence (*tajuyūshin*) appears in response
to the people's desire and benefits them through the
various teachings that they desire to hear. The Buddha's life, which is described in the "one chapter and
two halves" of the Lotus Sutra, refers to the life of the
Buddha who attained enlightenment at a specific point
in time called *gohyaku-jintengō*. In this sense, it falls
under the category of the Buddha of beneficence. In
contrast, the Buddha who embodies the Law to which
he was enlightened is originally endowed with the
Buddha's qualities and is called the Buddha of absolute
freedom. Nichiren Daishonin is the historical manifestation of this Buddha who revealed and spread the Law
so that all people can attain Buddhahood.

The concept of "one chapter and two halves" has two
interpretations: that of the Great Teacher T'ien-t'ai,
who systematized the twenty-eight-chapter Lotus Sutra and defined it as the core of the sutra, and that of
Nichiren Daishonin. According to T'ien-t'ai's interpretation, the latter half of the *Yujutsu* chapter begins with
Shakyamuni's statement that the Bodhisattvas of the
Earth are his disciples, implying his enlightenment in
the distant past. However, the Daishonin defines the

latter half of the *Yujutsu* chapter as beginning with Bodhisattva Miroku's second question concerning how
the Buddha contrived to teach so many bodhisattvas in
the short span of a few decades and his request that the
Buddha explain further for the sake of people in the
future. To sum up, from the viewpoint of Shakyamuni's
Buddhism, Shakyamuni Buddha is the teacher and the
Bodhisattvas of the Earth are his disciples. According to
the more profound interpretation, however, Nichiren
Daishonin begins the "one chapter and two halves"
with the section in which the Bodhisattvas of the Earth
are compared to centenarians and the Buddha is likened
to a young man of twenty-five years old. This implies
that the Bodhisattvas of the Earth are more venerable
than Shakyamuni.

19. General and Specific Transfers

IN the *Jinriki* (twenty-first) chapter of the Lotus Sutra,
Shakyamuni transfers the essence of the sutra to Bodhisattva Jōgyō and the other Bodhisattvas of the Earth,
entrusting them with its propagation after his passing.
This transfer is called the specific transmission because
it was made specifically to the Bodhisattvas of the
Earth. In contrast, the general transmission of the sutra
was made to all the assembled bodhisattvas in the subse-
quent *Zokurui* (twenty-second) chapter.

The transfer in the *Jinriki* chapter has a close connection with the ceremony in the *Yujutsu* (fifteenth) chapter in which Shakyamuni called forth the Bodhisattvas

of the Earth after declining the request of the other bodhisattvas who vowed to propagate the sutra. The reasons why Shakyamuni declined their request are as follows. These bodhisattvas from other worlds were not deeply versed in the Law which is to be propagated after Shakyamuni's death. Moreover, the age of its propagation is so defiled by the impurities of society and the people's propensities that they would not be able to persevere through hardships and persecutions in its undertaking. Accordingly, the general transfer made to them all in the *Zokurui* chapter implies that the Law and the age in which it is to be spread are different from those indicated in the *Jinriki* chapter.

The age referred to in the *Jinriki* chapter is the evil-ridden Latter Day of the Law when the people's minds are extremely defiled and distorted. The *Yakuō* (twenty-third) and *Fugen* (twenty-eighth) chapters define the age in the future as "the fifth five hundred years after my [Shakyamuni's] death." The fifth five hundred years is the last of the five five-hundred-year periods following Shakyamuni's death that are described in the *Dai-juku* Sutra (Sutra of the Great Assembly), which refers to the beginning of the Latter Day of the Law. Moreover, the Law which would be propagated in the Latter Day is the Mystic Law, implied in the "one chapter and two halves," especially in the *Juryō* (sixteenth) chapter, which states that all people have the capacity to attain enlightenment.

In the *Zokurui* chapter, on the other hand, Shakyamuni Buddha makes a general transfer of the Lotus Sutra to all the bodhisattvas. This was made in response to the sincerity with which they pledged to propagate the Buddha's teaching after his death in the *Kanji* (thirteenth) and *Anrakugyō* (fourteenth) chapters. In the *Kanji* chapter, the vow of these numerous bodhisattvas is stated in verse and is often called the "twenty-line verse," which enumerates the types of persecutions that will be met in propagating the sutra in the fearful latter age. Their leader was Bodhisattva Yakuō. They made a vow and expressed their determination to spread the sutra, regardless of what powerful enemies they might face. Although Shakyamuni rejected their request in the *Yujutsu* chapter, he entrusted them with the mission of propagating the sutra during the two thousand years of the Former and Middle Days of the Law following his death. By doing this, he responded to their sincere vow and determination. The Great Teacher T'ien-t'ai, who established the supremacy of the Lotus Sutra in the Middle Day, is therefore said to be a reincarnation of Bodhisattva Yakuō. Bodhisattva Jōgyō, who was entrusted with the spreading of the Mystic Law in the Latter Day, is the provisional or ephemeral figure of the original Buddha of *kuon ganjo,* who made his advent as Nichiren Daishonin, the Buddha of the Latter Day.

Part Four
History of Buddhism

1. Outline

AFTER Shakyamuni Buddha's passing, Buddhism was first propagated throughout India and then to the neighboring countries. It spread in two main directions. One was toward present-day Sri Lanka, Burma, Cambodia, Indonesia and other Southeast Asian countries. This division is called Southern Buddhism. Buddhism also spread through Central Asia to China and then to the Korean Peninsula and Japan. The teachings which proliferated in these countries are collectively referred to as Northern Buddhism.

Southern Buddhism basically followed and transmitted the tenets and rituals of early Buddhist teachings developed in India, even though to a certain degree it underwent changes influenced by the culture with regard to its externals. In contrast, Northern Buddhism not only was greatly influenced by national and cultural characteristics, but evolved and changed considerably in terms of its doctrines and rituals.

The principal stage on which Buddhism played its part during the one thousand years after Shakyamuni's death was India and Central Asia. In the first half-millennium, belief in Buddhism flourished particularly among monks and nuns in India, and it was a teaching based on those sutras that stressed adherence to precepts. The latter half-millennium was the period in which the spread of Buddhism centered around the Gandhāra region in the proximity of Central Asia. There, Buddhists emphasized philosophical pursuits and established higher systems of Buddhist theory such as the concept of non-substantiality (*kū*) and the Consciousness-Only doctrine. They called their Buddhism Mahayana (great vehicle), and they criticized the traditional, precept-centered schools, contemptuously labeling them Hinayana (lesser vehicle).

It is thought that the history of Buddhism in China began around five hundred years after Shakyamuni's death. (According to Buddhist tradition, Buddhism was brought to China about one thousand years after Shakyamuni's death, for the period of his lifetime is placed five hundred years earlier than the date suggested by modern scholars.) Nearly five hundred years after the introduction of Buddhism to China, the Great Teacher T'ien-t'ai made his advent and established the doctrine of *ichinen sanzen* on the basis of the Lotus Sutra. Not long after his appearance, Buddhism was introduced to Japan, and in its initial stage, the Lotus Sutra was greatly esteemed, although it was not accorded the highest place among Buddhist teachings. The Great Teacher Dengyō followed in T'ien-t'ai's steps and exerted himself in disseminating the teaching of *ichinen sanzen*. However, after his death, the lineage of the school based on the Lotus Sutra was cut and discontinued.

According to Buddhist tradition, the Latter Day of the Law, two thousand years after Shakyamuni's passing, was believed to have begun in the eleventh century. With many people having lost sight of the fact that Shakyamuni Buddha was the founder of Buddhism, new schools arose in succession, lauding the powers of imaginary Buddhas who appeared in the sutras or denying the need to pursue doctrinal studies or to carry out the practice of Buddhism. The true spirit of Buddhism had been all but lost by the beginning of the thirteenth century in Japan. In the midst of this atmosphere of confusion, Nichiren Daishonin made his appearance.

At about the same time, Buddhism in India suffered the impact of Islam from the west and disappeared, although it had earlier maintained a meager existence in conjunction with esotericism after the extinction of Shakyamuni's successors in the sixth century. Similarly, after the death of T'ien-t'ai, Buddhism in China fell into a state of disorder, eroded by the influence of Indian esotericism and the prevalence of Amida worship, a derivation of Buddhism itself. Moreover, the Mongol invasion of China in the thirteenth century caused the decline of Buddhism as a whole. During this period of gradual decline of Northern Buddhism, Nichiren Daishonin appeared and established the true teachings of Buddhism which would illuminate the darkness of the Latter Day of the Law.

2. Three Periods of Propagation

THE propagation of any religion can be divided into three periods according to the degree to which the people are influenced. During the first period, a religion can offer a practical means to solve actual problems confronting people. The second period is when the religion has become established within the culture and society, but becomes formalized and is no longer relevant to the needs of people. During the third period, the religion completely loses its effectiveness. These three stages are respectively called in Buddhism the Former Day of the Law, the Middle Day of the Law and the Latter Day of the Law.

According to Buddhist thought, the Former Day of the Law covered one thousand years; the Middle Day of the Law also lasted for one millennium. The following period, ten thousand years and more, is called the Latter Day of the Law. During the Former Day immediately following the death of Shakyamuni, Buddhism for the most part was practiced in India, but at the beginning of the Middle Day it spread to China. The sutras and treatises were translated into Chinese. Then, around the middle of this period, Buddhism spread through the Korean Peninsula to Japan. These are the generally accepted views concerning the Former and Middle Days, but it is also possible to divide the historical period of Buddhist propagation within each country into these three consecutive periods.

The Former Day, the Middle Day and the Latter Day cannot be exactly defined because opinion is divided as to precisely when Shakyamuni lived and died. However, according to Asian Buddhist tradition, Shakyamuni died in 949 B.C. Accordingly, the first year of the Latter Day would fall on A.D. 1052. The classification of the three periods does not indicate a change in the teaching itself, but rather is related to variations in the capacity of those people, especially Buddhist priests, who receive the teachings. During the initial stage of propagation, when the followers of Buddhism are still a minority within society, they base their practice on pure faith. However, with the acquisition of power, authority and wealth, the desire for fame and other ambitions arise and become prominent in their minds. Eventually, the leading priests of the Buddhist order lose their pure faith. At such a time, the religion may be said to have entered the phase of the Latter Day of the Law.

Buddhism all but died out in India and China. In Japan as well, learned priests became influenced by greed, anger and stupidity, and Shakyamuni's Buddhism entirely lost its power of redemption. In this evil age, Nichiren Daishonin made his advent as the Buddha who would reveal the way of enlightenment and save all people.

The concept of the Latter Day is based on the changes that were predicted to occur in Shakyamuni's Buddhism, but it can be equally applied to any religion—even Western religions such as Christianity. By observing the degree to which a religion can benefit its followers, it is possible to identify the period it is going through as the Former Day, the Middle Day or the Latter Day. Similarly, a time when any philosophy loses its power to enlighten and redeem humanity from despair, alienation and other problems can also be said to be undergoing changes equivalent to those of the Latter Day of the Law.

3. Origin of the Sutras

SHAKYAMUNI attained enlightenment at the age of thirty and expounded a great many teachings in accordance with the people's capacity and understanding. He continued to teach for fifty years and died at the age of eighty, yet his teachings still did not form a complete system of thought. They concerned the wisdom of life and attitudes in faith which were expounded according to his disciples' needs. Shakyamuni's enlightenment to the ultimate truth certainly underlay all of his teachings, but since he found that truth was inexpressible, he did not expound the ultimate truth itself.

After Shakyamuni's death, his teachings were orally transmitted by his disciples, and about one hundred years later they were recalled and organized according to content. However, many of the oral teachings were left unrecorded. For a few centuries thereafter, the memorized canon was recited in order to include the rest of the oral teachings and to keep them intact. According to Buddhist tradition, shortly after Shakyamuni Buddha's death, the First Buddhist Council was held to preserve the Buddha's teachings. A hundred years later saw the Second Buddhist Council, and two hundred years later the Third Council took place under the patronage of King Ashoka. Then, four hundred years after the Buddha's passing, the Fourth Council was carried out under the patronage of King Kanishka. Such is the traditional account, though when the Buddhist councils actually took place is difficult to determine. It seems quite possible that Shakyamuni's teachings were not recorded in sutra form until a very long time after his passing.

First of all, precepts were required to maintain discipline in the monastic orders. Consequently the Hinayana sutras, which center on precepts, were probably recorded before most other teachings. Later the Buddha's other teachings, free from complicated precepts, were widely propagated to the laity. The need for compiling them became increasingly urgent, and at that time the Mahayana sutras were written down. This event took place some time after Shakyamuni's death, though just when is hard to say. It is not clearly known precisely when Shakyamuni's teachings on the ultimate truth were compiled in the form of the Lotus Sutra. In the Gosho, Nichiren Daishonin states that the Lotus Sutra appeared immediately after Shakyamuni's death, and this seems most plausible. The magnificent Ceremony in the Air is employed in the Lotus Sutra to indicate Shakyamuni's enlightenment, the virtually inexpressible Mystic Law. Although what is written in the sutra is extremely difficult and profound, at the earliest stage of compiling and confirming the Buddha's teachings, the Lotus Sutra must have been valued most as the teaching that enables all people to attain enlightenment.

4. Mahayana and Hinayana

BUDDHISM developed in India, and there it divided into two main streams. One found its way into present-day Sri Lanka, Burma, Thailand and Indonesia, while the other spread via the Hindu Kush to Central Asia and then to China, the Korean Peninsula and Japan. The former system of belief is called Hinayana, and the latter, Mahayana.

According to Hinayana doctrines, sufferings are caused by desires and selfishness within human life. To eliminate suffering, Hinayana teachings urge people to extinguish all desires. For this reason those who follow Hinayana believe that to achieve a state of nothingness is the ideal, and that this ideal is called nirvana. However, to extinguish desire means to extinguish one's existence in this world, because desire is an intrinsic part of human life.

Both schools of thought attribute the cause of suffering to earthly desires, selfishness, etc., so there is no difference between Mahayana and Hinayana Buddhism in that regard. However, the Mahayana teaching denies the practice of extinguishing desire, encouraging one instead to manifest in oneself the universal life so that one can control desire and direct it positively, in this way abating suffering. On this point Mahayana Buddhism differs decisively from Hinayana.

The teachings of Mahayana Buddhism are subdivided into two parts. The first division postulates a transcendental being that people are taught to believe in.

These are called provisional Mahayana teachings, or teachings expounded before the Lotus Sutra. The idea of a transcendental being in provisional Mahayana has some similarity with ideas in Christianity or Islam, but there are differences. Provisional Mahayana teaches that a Buddha of perfect enlightenment exists in a paradise far away in another part of the universe and that believers can travel to the land of this transcendental being after their death. In Christianity and Islam, the supreme being, transcending the dimensions of this phenomenal world, controls and governs it.

The second division of Mahayana Buddhism, which consists of the Lotus Sutra, identifies, in contrast to a transcendental being, a universal self that exists simultaneously within one's own life, within this phenomenal world and throughout the universe. In Christianity and pre-Lotus Sutra teachings this universal self, or ultimate reality, is visualized in terms of a "personality." The Lotus Sutra, however, regards this reality as a "law" which governs everything. Nichiren Daishonin identified the law as Nam-myoho-renge-kyo.

If people are faithful to the teachings of Hinayana Buddhism and act accordingly, they must deny existence in this world. Even people who follow the provisional Mahayana teachings will certainly attempt to escape from daily life and society rather than living within it. In contrast, the Lotus Sutra, as interpreted by Nichiren Daishonin, established the way to challenge the sufferings and problems of society and to reform this trouble-ridden world, not by escaping from it, but by positively living among the people. Its teachings show the way to freedom from selfishness and self-righteousness and the way to genuine human fulfillment based upon the universal self.

5. Successors of Buddhism in India

JUST as Shakyamuni is said to have predicted, twenty-four people successively inherited the lineage of his Buddhism and propagated it in India during the one thousand years of the Former Day of the Law. They are called the twenty-four successors.

The first, Mahākāshyapa, and the second, Ānanda, received the Buddha's teachings directly from him. The successors from Mahākāshyapa through the sixth successor, Dhritaka, appeared during the one hundred years after Shakyamuni's death and spread Hinayana Buddhism exclusively. During the ensuing four hundred years, the seventh successor, Mikkaka, through the eleventh, Punyayashas, chiefly propagated Hinayana teachings, but with some ingredients of Mahayana intermixed. In the following five hundred years thirteen successors, from Ashvaghosha, the twelfth, through Nāgārjuna, the fourteenth, to Āryasimha, the twenty-fourth successor, denounced Hinayana and spread Mahayana teachings exclusively. Among these twenty-four successors of Shakyamuni, Ashvaghosha, Nāgārjuna, Āryadeva, the fifteenth, Vasubandhu, the twenty-first, and Āryasimha are especially known for their outstanding achievements.

During the first one hundred years, Buddhism spread in the northeastern part of India, near the Ganges River, and centered primarily on a group of monks. Therefore, great emphasis was placed on monastic precepts, and Hinayana Buddhism was propagated exclusively. During the following four hundred years, as is reflected in the conversion of King Ashoka, Buddhism spread throughout almost all of India and lay Buddhists made up a considerable percentage of the population. Accordingly, Hinayana was disseminated as the principal teaching, mixed with some elements of what would later become Mahayana. The latter five hundred years of the Former Day of the Law, beginning with Ashvaghosha, saw the exclusive propagation of Mahayana. Buddhism spread as far as the northern part of present-day Afghanistan, an area in Central Asia. In the eastern and southern parts of India, however, Hinayana Buddhism maintained a steady influence, notwithstanding the prosperity of Mahayana Buddhism, and laid a foundation for Southern Buddhism, which would later make its way into the Southeast Asian countries.

The expansion and prosperity of Mahayana was mainly due to such powerful patrons of Buddhism as King Kanishka who made a great contribution to the flowering of Gandhāra culture in northern India, the region adjoining Central Asia. Ashvaghosha was held in high esteem by King Kanishka. One may suppose that all the people in India embraced Buddhism during these latter five hundred years. This was not so, however. Even as Buddhism grew and flourished, Brahmanism still retained tremendous influence in society.

There are episodes that indicate that Ashvaghosha and Nāgārjuna carried out untiring practices in order to convert kings who adhered to Brahmanism.* Moreover, Āryadeva was killed by a disciple of a Brahman teacher, and Āryasimha, the last of the twenty-four successors, was beheaded by a king who upheld Brahmanism and attacked Buddhism. Thereafter, Buddhism in India underwent a process of transformation and degeneration under the influence of esotericism. Eventually it fused with Hinduism, an advanced form of Brahmanism, and ceased to exist as a separate religion in India. The center of Mahayana Buddhism had by this time moved northeast via Central Asia to China.

6. Achievements of the Mahayana Scholars

NOTEWORTHY among Shakyamuni's twenty-four successors are Ashvaghosha, the twelfth, Nāgārjuna, the fourteenth, and Vasubandhu, the twenty-first successor. Nichiren Daishonin often refers to these scholars in his writings. Ashvaghosha paved the way for the rise of Mahayana thought, Nāgārjuna achieved fame by firmly

---

*Ashvagosha was offered by his king to an enemy state in lieu of a huge sum demanded in tribute by the enemy. But he did not lose heart; instead he remained remarkably active and made northern India, the land of his captivity, a stage for propagating the Buddhist Law. Nāgārjuna, in order to convert his king, is said to have walked back and forth in front of the palace, bearing a red flag, for seven years. His curiosity aroused by such actions, the king summoned Nāgārjuna for a meeting. Nāgārjuna then refuted the heretical teachings and awakened the king to the Buddhist Law.

establishing its concepts, and Vasubandhu developed these theoretical basis still further.

Ashvaghosha, a second-century scholar, was born in Shrāvastī in central India, where Shakyamuni had frequently gone to preach. He first studied Brahmanism and loudly denounced Buddhism. However, he was later converted by Pārshva, the tenth of the twenty-four successors, and led many people to the Buddha's teachings through his skill in poetry and literature. He is said to have once converted five hundred princes to Buddhism with a drama he wrote. Furthermore, he converted King Kanishka, when the latter invaded Shrāvastī, and accompanied him to northern India. With the support of King Kanishka, he propagated Mahayana there and caused it to flourish.

Nāgārjuna was born to a Brahman family in southern India and lived between A.D. 150 and 250. He at first studied Hinayana Buddhism but later converted to Mahayana. He wrote treatises on a great number of Mahayana sutras and established the theoretical foundation of Mahayana thought, thus making an inestimable contribution to its development. Since his doctrine is integral to Mahayana Buddhism, Nāgārjuna is revered as the founder of the eight sects (Kusha, Jōjitsu, Ritsu, Hossō, Sanron, Kegon, Tendai and Shingon). The most representative work attributed to him is the *Daichido ron* (Treatise on the Sutra of the Perfection of Wisdom) which became the basis of many later Mahayana doctrines.

Vasubandhu is thought to have lived around the fourth or fifth century. Born in Gandhāra in northern India, he studied Hinayana Buddhism and compiled such works as the *Kusha ron* (A Treasury of Analyses of the Law), which presented a theoretical basis for later Hinayana thought. However, influenced by his elder brother, Asanga, he later converted to Mahayana. He wrote many Mahayana works and contributed greatly to the prosperity of Mahayana. His Consciousness-Only doctrine, in particular, later evolved into the concept of the nine consciousnesses.

These scholars upheld and worked with Mahayana scriptures other than the Lotus Sutra. The reason is that the pre-Lotus Sutra Mahayana teachings were those which were to be propagated during the one thousand years of the Former Day of the Law following Shakyamuni's death. The spread of the Lotus Sutra itself had to await the appearance of the Great Teacher T'ien-t'ai in the Middle Day of the Law. Nichiren Daishonin conjectures that, although not qualified to spread the Lotus Sutra firsthand, these scholars based their speculations on that sutra, and that they were awakened to the ultimate Law hidden in the depths of the *Juryō* (sixteenth) chapter of the sutra, that is, Nam-myoho-renge-kyo. For example, Nāgārjuna's teachings were all-encompassing, so he was respected as the founder of various sects and schools that later branched out in India, China and Japan. It is conceivable, therefore, that underlying what he expounded was his enlightenment to the universal truth, which allowed him to integrate all the seemingly conflicting doctrines.

7. Buddhism in China

MAHAYANA Buddhism flourished in Gandhāra, north-ern part of present-day Afghanistan, and found its way east via the Silk Road, finally reaching China. It is docu-mented that Buddhism was introduced into China soon after the beginning of the Christian era. However, Buddhism was probably first transmitted to some areas of China a few centuries before that.

Confucianism and Taoism were already established in China by then. The teachings of Confucius (551–479 B.C.) stressed the need for the order and harmony of human relationships in this life. However, the Chinese rulers paid little attention to Confucius's admonitions, and his doctrines had hardly any practical effect during his day. It was during the Han dynasty that his teach-ings were finally given recognition, becoming a state philosophy and later almost a state religion. Taoism is based on the teachings of Lao Tzu, about whom little is known. It highly values life which is in harmony with nature and noninterference with the course of natural events.

Buddhism inevitably underwent changes within the Chinese spiritual environment and made surprising new developments. In India, Buddhism had not yet been formulated into a philosophical system, but after being transmitted to China it was systematized, as Con-fucianism had been earlier. However, in the process of lending order or systematizing the entire collection of scriptures, a wide variety of opinions arose as to the question of which sutra or sutras were most profound and contained the true intention of Shakyamuni Buddha. This led to controversy. In the fifth and sixth centuries, there were a number of established sects, commonly referred to as the three schools south of the Yangtze River and seven schools north of the river. The Great Teacher T'ien-t'ai appeared and organized all of the innumerable Buddhist sutras by formulating a system of classification. He refuted the conclusions of the earlier schools and established the supremacy of the Lotus Sutra. In addition, there were several schools of Buddhism which came under the influence of popular Taoist thinking. Those Buddhist schools also enjoyed great popularity.

Reviewing the history of Buddhism in China from the first century through the eighth century, we find that, in spite of great hardships and difficulties, many Chinese priests went to India to seek the Buddhist teachings and, in turn, many Indian priests went to China. They dedicated themselves to the introduction and translation of Buddhist scriptures. In China, faith in the Lotus Sutra spread mainly as a result of the Chinese translation made by Kumārajīva (344–413), who lived prior to T'ien-t'ai. T'ien-t'ai established the profound doctrine of Buddhism on the basis of the *Myoho-renge-kyo,* the Chinese translation of the Lotus Sutra made by Kumārajīva. Nichiren Daishonin, considering it the best among the Chinese translations of the Lotus Sutra, used it to explain his teaching.

8. The Great Teacher T'ien-t'ai

T'IEN-T'AI's name is Chih-i, and his title is the Great Teacher Chih-che (the Wise). He is commonly called the Great Teacher T'ien-t'ai because his primary base of activities was on Mt. T'ien-t'ai in southern China.

His thought and practice were based on Shakya-muni's teachings, particularly the *Myoho-renge-kyo,* Kumārajīva'a translation of the Lotus Sutra. In a broad sense, however, he pursued his studies of Buddhism on the basis of Nāgārjuna's teachings. Hui-wen and Hui-ssu are the teachers who brought T'ien-t'ai closer to the core of the Lotus Sutra. Under the guidance of Hui-ssu (later called the Great Teacher Nan-yüeh), T'ien-t'ai exerted himself in Buddhist practice in order to grasp the essence of the sutra. He is said to have finally attained an awakening at the age of twenty-three. In those days, southern China was ruled by a succession of dynasties. T'ien-t'ai received the support of the emperor of the Ch'en dynasty, and expounded his teachings to him. He was also revered by Emperor Yang of the Sui dynasty, who unified all of China under his rule. He was given the title of the Great Teacher Chih-che by this emperor.

T'ien-t'ai's achievements may be divided into two major categories. One is the fact that he organized the vast number of Buddhist sutras into five periods and eight teachings. Through this system, he revealed that the Lotus Sutra is the highest among all of Shakya-muni's teachings, and thereby refuted the views of the many other schools prevalent in China at the time, which had disputed over the question of which sutra or sutras contained the true intention of Shakyamuni Buddha. The other is the fact that, on the basis of the Lotus Sutra, he formulated the doctrine of *ichinen san-zen* (three thousand realms in a single moment of life) as the ultimate principle of Buddhism.

The five periods is a classification of the Buddhist sutras according to the order in which they were expounded, consisting of the Kegon, Agon, Hōdō, Hannya and Hokke-Nehan periods. The eight teachings organizes Shakyamuni's teachings according to content and method of presentation. It consists of two subclassifications—the four teachings of doctrine, made up of the Tripitaka teaching, the connecting teaching, the specific teaching and the perfect teaching; and the four teachings of method, which consist of the sudden teaching, the gradual teaching, the secret teaching and the indeterminate teaching. Through this classification of the five periods and eight teachings, T'ien-t'ai determined the relative superiority of all the sutras and where within the entire system each scripture should belong. As a result, he established the supremacy of the Lotus Sutra, and claimed that all the other sutras are preparatory teachings designed to increase the people's capacity to understand the Buddha's ultimate teaching as revealed in the Lotus Sutra.

The ultimate purpose of Buddhist practice is to realize that all phenomena, or the three thousand possible conditions, are integrated in a single moment of life, and that Buddhahood is inherent in all life. Herein lies the true significance of the doctrine of *ichinen sanzen*. But one must transcend ordinary intellectual understanding in order to grasp it, and the practices needed to do so are so arduous and the doctrine itself so difficult that most ordinary people were unable to arrive at a correct realization of the truth. Nichiren Daishonin rendered the principle of *ichinen sanzen* into concrete form as the Gohonzon and established its practice as the invocation of the daimoku, thereby opening the way for all people to attain Buddhahood. It may be said, therefore, that from the viewpoint of Nichiren Daishonin's Buddhism, T'ien-t'ai's doctrine of *ichinen sanzen* was a blueprint for the inscription of the Gohonzon. For this reason, the Gohonzon is called actual *ichinen sanzen,* and the *ichinen sanzen* as set forth in T'ien-t'ai's Buddhism is called theoretical *ichinen sanzen.*

9. Buddhism in Japan

DURING the sixth century A.D. Buddhism was transmitted to Japan through Korea. In those days Japan had no other religious system as such, but followed the practices of ancestor worship and nature worship. Before the Japanese finally accepted Buddhism, their country was torn by strife among the major clans over the question of whether to accept this new religion or not. Eventually, Buddhism and the worship of the native Shinto gods came to coexist, a situation similar to that in China, where Buddhism, Confucianism and Taoism all existed together. The native deities were incorporated into the philosophical system of Buddhism as Buddhist gods, just as the gods indigenous to India were amalgamated with Buddhism. In a somewhat similar way, Christianity adopted various ways of thinking and ceremonies from earlier faiths as well as concepts characteristic of Greek philosophy. Both Buddhism and Christianity incorporated ideas or concepts from other faiths or philosophical systems, though Buddhism has shown greater flexibility in this respect than Christianity.

In Japan Buddhism became the spiritual basis of the nation. Prince Shōtoku, who was a regent of the empress, formally recognized the Lotus Sutra and other Mahayana sutras as teachings which could protect and unify the country. Emperor Shōmu built many state-sponsored provincial temples for priests and nuns throughout the country, and Tōdai-ji temple in the capital of Nara was the headquarters of them all. The Lotus Sutra and the *Konkōmyō* Sutra (Sutra of the Golden Light) were held in great esteem by the temples, and in temples for nuns the Lotus Sutra was valued more highly than any other sutra. This was because the sutra teaches that both men and women can attain Buddhahood equally, while the other sutras deny women the possibility of Buddhahood. Gradually Buddhism began to spread throughout the population on the basis of belief in the Lotus Sutra.

Although at first the temples were not affiliated with any specific sects, later, as more sutras were brought to Japan from China, Hinayana sects, which stressed adherence to precepts, were established. Buddhism changed from a virtual state religion to a sect-based religion. Faith in the Lotus Sutra, which the Great Teacher Dengyō fortified with T'ien-t'ai's Buddhist philosophy, underwent a great revival. However, as time passed, the esoteric teaching and practice of the Shingon sect became more influential, superseding the teaching of the Lotus Sutra in popularity. The Jōdo (Pure Land) sect attracted many followers, turning people's hopes toward salvation in the next life, and in time came to exert a great influence on the people.

Toward the end of the Heian period (794–1185) the samurai took over political power, replacing the emperor and the court nobles as the real rulers of the country. Samurai originally appeared from among the farming class. From this time through the Kamakura period (1185–1333), Buddhist sects such as the Jōdo and Zen sects, which required no understanding of profound Buddhist doctrines, rose and became popular among the people.

It was in these days of religious and social ferment that Nichiren Daishonin made his advent. Taking the doctrines of T'ien-t'ai and Dengyō as his starting point, he presented his Buddhism in a way that made it easy for ordinary people to understand and put into practice. It goes beyond the framework of Chinese Buddhism, which had surpassed the limitations of the Indian ways of thinking, and it has the power to find its way into the hearts of all the people of the world.

10. Characteristics of Buddhist Sects in Japan

THERE are a great many Buddhist sects in Japan today. History has witnessed the rise and fall of many of them. A brief outline of them will be given here in order to pave the way for a better understanding of Nichiren Daishonin's writings, the Gosho.

During the Nara period (710–794), six schools of Buddhism flourished in Nara, the capital of Japan at that time. They are the Kegon, Hossō, Kusha, Jōjitsu, Ritsu and Sanron sects. Those who pursued the study of Buddhism went from one school to the other, and exerted themselves in Buddhist practice under their own teachers. However, it was not long before these sects began contending with one another in an attempt to expand their spheres of influence. When the Great Teacher Dengyō founded the Tendai sect on the basis of the Lotus Sutra, they all tried to attack it. Among these early sects, the Kegon, Hossō and Ritsu are still extant as independent religious sects, but their influence is extremely weak.

At the beginning of the Heian period (794–1185), the Tendai sect was established by Dengyō, and the Shingon sect was founded by Kōbō (also called Kūkai). The Shingon sect bases its doctrine on the *Dainichi* (Mahāvairochana) Sutra. Kōbō did not denounce the Lotus Sutra openly while Dengyō was alive, but after Dengyō's death, Kōbō claimed that the Lotus Sutra was inferior to the *Dainichi* and *Kegon* (Flower Garland) sutras. He ingratiated himself with those in power in order to broaden his influence. Eventually, even chief priests of the Tendai sect fell under Shingon's influence and became instilled with the erroneous doctrines of Shingon esotericism. The Tendai sect, mixed with esoteric teachings, is called Tendai esotericism (Taimitsu). In contrast, the Shingon sect in the direct line of Kōbō is called eastern esotericism (Tōmitsu), because its headquarters is at Tō-ji (Eastern Temple) in Kyoto. In several of his writings, Nichiren Daishonin deplores the stupidity of the chief priests of the Tendai sect who were led to corrupt Dengyō's teachings.

Toward the end of the Heian period, Hōnen founded the Jōdo (Pure Land), or Nembutsu, sect and stressed the practice of reciting the name of Amida Buddha as the only means by which to attain rebirth in the Pure Land. Moreover, the Zen teachings, brought to Japan by Chinese priests, were established as a sect in the Kamakura period (1185–1333). This sect urged people to seek enlightenment through the practice of seated meditation without the pursuit of doctrinal studies or the recitation of sutras. The six sects of Nara, plus the Tendai and Shingon sects, are collectively referred to as the eight sects, and the eight sects plus the Nembutsu and Zen sects are often referred to as the ten major sects of Japanese Buddhism in the Gosho.

The eight sects in general attached greater importance to the pursuit of doctrinal studies. Therefore, Nichiren Daishonin himself went to the temples of these sects in the Kyoto and Nara areas during the initial stage of his study of Buddhism. In the period from the proclamation of his Buddhism in 1253 until the Tatsunokuchi Persecution in 1271, the Daishonin mainly denounced the beliefs of the Jōdo and Zen sects, which were most widespread among the ordinary people at that time. He deeply grieved that many people were destined to fall into hell because they put their faith in these misleading tenets. This misfortune was due to the people's ignorance of Buddhist doctrines. In terms of the "fivefold comparison," the Daishonin's refutation was made on the level of a comparison between provisional Mahayana (the pre-Lotus Sutra Mahayana teachings) and true Mahayana (the Lotus Sutra). After the Tatsunokuchi Persecution, he clarified the superiority of the Buddhism of sowing (Nichiren Daishonin's Buddhism) over the Buddhism of the harvest (Shakyamuni's Buddhism), and attacked the Shingon and Tendai sects. The reason is that although both sects studied the Lotus Sutra and upheld the doctrine of theoretical *ichinen sanzen,* an abstract philosophical system, they failed to realize actual *ichinen sanzen,* the only way to attain Buddhahood in the Latter Day of the Law. In the final analysis, Nichiren Daishonin refuted the erroneous views of these various sects as part of the process of expounding his own teachings, as well as revealing his role in the course of the history of Buddhism.

11. Nikkō Shonin

SHORTLY before Nichiren Daishonin passed away, he took steps to designate Nikkō Shonin (1246–1333) as his legitimate successor. Having thus, in two transfer documents, entrusted all of his teachings to Nikkō Shonin, the Daishonin passed away on October 13, 1282, at Ike-gami in present-day Tokyo. In the transfer documents, the Daishonin states plainly that Nikkō Shonin should lead in the propagation of the Daishonin's teachings and become the chief priest of Kuon-ji temple in Minobu.

Nikkō Shonin was one of the Daishonin's six senior disciples, and was the third among them in the order of conversion. He had become the Daishonin's disciple when he was thirteen years old, an acolyte pursuing his studies. Later, while accompanying the Daishonin during some of his severest trials, such as the Izu and Sado exiles, Nikkō Shonin heard many of the Daisho-nin's most important teachings firsthand. For this rea-son, and because of his strong faith and excellent understanding, Nikkō Shonin correctly perceived the true nature of the Daishonin's identity and intentions.

Nikkō Shonin returned to Minobu after the Daisho-nin's passing to take up the responsibilities of chief priest. At this point the other five senior priests re-turned to the regions around Japan where they were directing propagation activities. Although they shared responsibility with Nikkō Shonin on a rotating basis for attending to the Daishonin's tomb, none of them re-turned to carry out his duty.

Furthermore, misunderstanding the true significance of the Daishonin's Buddhism, they became estranged from Nikkō Shonin, and even, to protect themselves from persecution, began to identify themselves as priests of the long-established Tendai sect.

Meanwhile, Nikkō Shonin appointed Nikō, one of the five senior priests, who had returned to Minobu, as the head of studies. However, Nikō persisted in his wrong ideas, and, under his influence, the steward of the Minobu area, Hakiri Sanenaga, took to disobeying the Daishonin's teachings; he then ignored all of Nikkō Shonin's instructions to desist in this behavior.

At this point, in the spring of 1289, Nikkō Shonin, convinced that at Minobu he could no longer properly protect the true teachings of Buddhism, left the area with his followers, bearing with him the Dai-Gohon-zon, the Daishonin's ashes and other treasures.

When he arrived in Ueno Village near Mt. Fuji, the steward of the village, Nanjō Tokimitsu, also a lay follower of Nikkō Shonin, not only offered him temporary residence, but shortly thereafter offered a nearby tract of land at the foot of Mt. Fuji. This was the very sort of place Nichiren Daishonin had indicated in his writings as the best site on which to build the center for the spread of Buddhism. Here, in October 1290, Nikkō Shonin, with the help of his followers, completed a temple, which marked the beginning of Taiseki-ji.

From this moment on, Nikkō Shonin concentrated all his efforts on collecting the Daishonin's writings, promoting his teachings, educating disciples, advancing propagation and remonstrating with officials of the government.

In January 1333, shortly before his death, Nikkō Shonin wrote the "Nikkō yuikai okimon" (Twenty-six Admonitions of Nikkō), which includes the well-known article: "Until *kōsen-rufu* is achieved, propagate the Law to the full extent of your ability without begrudging your life." Then, after appointing Nichimoku Shonin as high priest of Taiseki-ji, Nikkō Shonin passed away on February 7, 1333, at the age of eighty-eight.

12. Nichikan Shonin

NICHIKAN Shonin (1665–1726), the twenty-sixth high priest of Taiseki-ji, is revered as a restorer of Nichiren Daishonin's Buddhism. His works are indispensable in the study of the Daishonin's teachings. During the time from the end of the seventeenth century through the beginning of the eighteenth century, when he lived, arbitrary interpretations arising from the various Nichiren sects were widespread and the true spirit of the Daishonin's teachings was in danger of disappearing completely. Nichikan Shonin sharply refuted these errors and misconceptions, and worked tirelessly to clarify the correct interpretation of the Daishonin's teachings.

At the age of forty-seven, Nichikan Shonin was appointed the chief instructor of Taiseki-ji and contributed to the promotion of the study of the Daishonin's Buddhism. He became the twenty-sixth high priest at the age of fifty-four, and two years later, turned over his position to Nichiyō Shonin, the twenty-seventh high priest, in order to devote his full energies to study. Nichiyō Shonin passed away three years later, however, so Nichikan Shonin again assumed the responsibility of high priest. Throughout his life, he devoted himself to the study of the Daishonin's teachings.

His achievements may be classified into two categories. One is his exegeses on Nichiren Daishonin's major writings, such as "The True Object of Worship," "The Opening of the Eyes" and the "Risshō ankoku ron." He provided each of these writings with the correct interpretation and clarified the Buddhist principles contained in them. The other category is represented by the *Rokkan shō,* or Six-volume Writings, a collection of six treatises. These are "Sanjū hiden shō" (The Threefold Secret Teaching), "Montei hichin shō" (Meanings Hidden in the Depths), "Egi hammon shō" (Interpretations Based on the Law), "Mappō sōō shō" (Teachings for the Latter Day), "Tōryū gyōji shō" (The Practice of This School) and "Tōke sanne shō" (The Three Robes of This School). The first three treatises concern doctrine, and the latter three deal with formalities.

"Sanjū hiden shō" explains that the Daishonin's doctrine of actual *ichinen sanzen,* or Nam-myoho-renge-kyo of the Three Great Secret Laws, lies not in any of the pre-Lotus Sutra teachings, but in the Lotus Sutra, more precisely in the depths of the *Juryō* (sixteenth) chapter of the essential teaching. "Montei hichin shō" discusses in detail the Three Great Secret Laws—the object of worship, the daimoku and the high sanctuary of true Buddhism. "Egi hammon shō" interprets important passages of the Lotus Sutra from the in-depth viewpoint of Nichiren Daishonin's Buddhism and identifies the Lotus Sutra as the sutra which serves to clarify the Three Great Secret Laws. "Mappō sōō shō" sets forth the correct object of worship to be established in the Latter Day of the Law, and "Tōryū gyōji shō" explains why the *Hōben* (second) and *Juryō* chapters are recited in gongyo. "Tōke sanne shō" explains the origin and significance of the traditional robe, the surplice and the prayer beads of the priesthood.

The sects which Nichikan Shonin refuted are now on the decline, and his work may therefore include discussions which are inapplicable for Buddhist practice today. Nevertheless, it has never lost its value as an important text for a correct understanding of Nichiren Daishonin's Buddhism.

13. The Soka Gakkai

THE Soka Gakkai was founded in 1930 by Tsunesaburō Makiguchi, who became its first president, and his disciple, Jōsei Toda. Although the organization was based on faith in Buddhism as taught by Nichiren Daishonin, at first it was a society of educators who studied and put into practice Makiguchi's Soka (value-creative) pedagogy. Thus it was named the Soka Kyōiku Gakkai (Value-Creating Education Society).

Its membership increased steadily and had reached three thousand by the time the Second World War was drawing to a close. In 1943, however, because of their opposition to the military government's coercive religious policy and thought control, twenty-one leaders of the organization, including President Makiguchi and General Director Toda, were arrested and imprisoned. On November 18, 1944, Makiguchi died in prison at the age of seventy-three. Toda was released in July 1945 and set out to rebuild the organization under the name Soka

Gakkai. Toda became the second president on May 3, 1951, and determined, at the same time, to expand the membership of the Soka Gakkai to 750,000 households. By 1957, Toda had achieved his goal.

Toda had an experience while in prison, which he later described in his autobiographical novel, *The Human Revolution*. The novel states that he experienced two kinds of realization. During his imprisonment, his thoughts were for a long time occupied by a question relating to the meaning of the Lotus Sutra's prologue, the *Muryōgi* Sutra (Sutra of Infinite Meaning). This sutra reads, ". . . his [the Buddha's] body neither existing nor not existing, neither caused or conditioned, neither self or other, neither square or round, neither short or long . . ."* He asked himself, "What does the Buddha's body mean? What actually is the Buddha?" After abundant daimoku and profound contemplation, he realized that the Buddha is life itself.

Another question he struggled to answer was: What is the truth of the Lotus Sutra? In mid-November 1944, while chanting daimoku in prison, he visualized the solemn Ceremony in the Air and saw himself participating as a Bodhisattva of the Earth. He also attained a great awakening to his mission of propagating the supreme Law as a disciple of Nichiren Daishonin.

These two experiences of Toda have great significance. The first experience is the starting point for the Soka Gakkai's movement to enable people to understand Buddhism in a relevant way as a "life philosophy." This is the philosophical basis of the Soka Gakkai. Toda's awakening to the mission of *kōsen-rufu* became

*See footnote on p. 49.

the prime point of all Soka Gakkai activities. This is the origin of the Soka Gakkai's conviction that its mission lies in accomplishing *kōsen-rufu* as followers of Nichiren Daishonin.

On May 3, 1960, Daisaku Ikeda, who had struggled alongside Toda and received training from him over the course of a decade, became the third president. He immediately set about propagating the Daishonin's teachings overseas, and it eventually spread to 115 countries. Under his leadership, the membership surged to more than eleven million people throughout the world. The Soka Gakkai International (SGI) was established in January 1975, and Ikeda was elected its president. He greatly expanded his efforts to create a global understanding of the Daishonin's Buddhism through the SGI's manifold activities to promote peace, culture and education.

Part Five
Principles for Practice

1. Outline

IN the Gosho "The Opening of the Eyes," Nichiren Daishonin states, "When it comes to understanding the Lotus Sutra, I have only a minute fraction of the vast ability that T'ien-t'ai and Dengyō possessed. But in my ability to endure persecution and the wealth of my compassion for others, I believe I would put them to shame."* T'ien-t'ai and Dengyō, both great masters of Buddhism, had already made a philosophical analysis of the Buddhist teachings and arrived at their full understanding on the basis of the Lotus Sutra. The Buddhism which Nichiren Daishonin lived with his entire being and established for the sake of all people aims at giving practical expression to the core of Buddhism, enabling them to attain Buddhahood. In short, the Daishonin's Buddhism is none other than the "Buddhism of actuality" which attaches importance to practice above all.

Then, what and how should one practice in order to reach enlightenment? Two of the most important principles in Nichiren Daishonin's Buddhism are the Three

*Major Writings, vol. 2, p. 118.

Great Secret Laws and the five guides for propagation. The Three Great Secret Laws reveal the entity of the Law which one practices, while the five guides are criteria which one must correctly understand in carrying out the practice. Nichiren Daishonin himself proclaims in "The Teaching, Capacity, Time and Country," "If one takes the five considerations outlined above into account when propagating the Buddhist Law, then one can surely become a teacher to the entire nation of Japan."* Nichikan Shonin, the twenty-sixth high priest of Taiseki-ji, also stresses this in his "Egi hammon shō" (Interpretations Based on the Law) by saying, "The Three Great Secret Laws should be propagated in accordance with the five guides." Thus, the five guides must be taken into account in the practice of propagating Buddhism.

Buddhism has traditionally held that the ultimate Law of the Buddha's enlightenment is too profound and remote to be explained in words, much less materialized in concrete form. The teachings expounded in a vast number of sutras, the doctrines unfolded by many scholars, and the rituals and methods of practice established by many schools—all have been regarded as ways to approach this ultimate Law. Moreover, it has been thought that the ultimate Law itself exists far apart from all phenomena.

Nichiren Daishonin identified the ultimate Law as Nam-myoho-renge-kyo of the Three Great Secret Laws—the Law hidden in the depths of the *Juryō* (sixteenth) chapter of the Lotus Sutra which is the highest of all Shakyamuni's teachings. He also indicated that

Major Writings, vol. 4, p. 13.

Nam-myoho-renge-kyo is the Law to which a few people, such as Nāgārjuna, Vasubandhu, T'ien-t'ai and Dengyō, became enlightened at the innermost depths of their lives through practices and speculations on all the Buddhist teachings, after Shakyamuni's passing. The Three Great Secret Laws consist of the object of worship, the high sanctuary and the invocation or daimoku, of true Buddhism. The object of worship means that the object to revere must be the supreme, ultimate Buddha, that is, the original Buddha of absolute freedom from time without beginning. The high sanctuary signifies the land of this supreme Buddha, and the daimoku is the name and teaching of this Buddha. Fundamentally, the Three Great Secret Laws are included in the object of worship. In other words, the object of faith and practice encompasses all Three Great Secret Laws within itself, and is therefore also called the One Great Secret Law.

Furthermore, the object of worship, or the basis of one's faith and practice, is viewed from the two aspects of the Person and the Law. In terms of the Person, the object includes all Buddhas and bodhisattvas, and in terms of the Law, all laws operating in the universe. The daimoku, or the form of one's practice to the object of worship, includes the aspects of both faith and practice. Faith encompasses all forms of contemplation, while practice involves all types of practice. The high sanctuary, or the effect of one's faith and practice, means places where the Dai-Gohonzon, as well as all Gohonzon, transcriptions of the Dai-Gohonzon, is enshrined. *Kaidan,* the Japanese word for sanctuary, originally meant an ordination platform where one vows to observe the monastic precepts. The purpose of keeping Buddhist precepts is "to stem injustice and stop evil" within oneself, thereby manifesting an indestructible state of life which never yields to any obstacle. Accordingly, the high sanctuary means places where one can enjoy boundless benefits through one's faith in and practice directed to the object of worship. Thus, the Three Great Secret Laws constitute the essense of Buddhism, integrating all Buddhist teachings, practices and benefits within themselves.

Nichiren Daishonin entrusted his followers with the mission of propagating the Buddhism of the Three Great Secret Laws to all people everywhere, as well as practicing it themselves. It is not too much to say that one qualification for the Buddha's disciples lies in carrying out this mission. In "Letter to Jakunichi-bō," he states, "Those who become Nichiren's disciples and followers should realize the profound karmic relationship they share with him and spread the Lotus Sutra in the same spirit."* In every part of his writings, he calls on all his followers to propagate his teachings.

Moreover, the Daishonin defines the fundamental elements of Buddhist practice as "faith, practice and study." In "The True Entity of Life," he states, "Believe in the Gohonzon, the supreme object of worship in the world. . . . Exert yourself in the two ways of practice and study. Without practice and study, there can be no Buddhism. You must not only persevere yourself; you must also teach others. Both practice and study arise from faith. Teach others to the best of your ability, even

*Major Writings, vol. 1, p. 236.

if [it be] only a single sentence or phrase."* As is clear from this statement, practice and study alone are not enough; one must teach and propagate the Daishonin's Buddhism. The five guides are criteria that must be taken into account in the altruistic practice of propagation.

In this chapter, the fundamental principles for the practice of Nichiren Daishonin's teachings, or the Buddhism of actuality, will be discussed in greater detail.

2. The Three Great Secret Laws

NICHIREN Daishonin established an eternal foundation for his teachings with the Three Great Secret Laws. These three comprise the Gohonzon, which is the object of worship, daimoku or the invocation of Nam-myoho-renge-kyo, and the high sanctuary, which is the place of practice. They are called "secret" because they transcend the understanding of ordinary people and because neither Shakyamuni nor his successors in India and China ever revealed them. They constitute the core of Buddhism revealed for the first time by Nichiren Daishonin.

This does not mean, however, that Shakyamuni, Nāgārjuna and T'ien-t'ai were unaware of these teachings. They were very much enlightened to Nam-myoho-renge-kyo. They also realized that the object of worship, the invocation and the high sanctuary were an

*Ibid., pp. 94–95.

integral part of belief and practice. There are, more-over, many passages in the Lotus Sutra which indicate the Three Great Secret Laws.

As Nichiren Daishonin states in "Sandai hihō shō" (On the Three Great Secret Laws) and other Gosho, the Three Great Secret Laws constitute the doctrine hidden in the depths of the *Juryō* (sixteenth) chapter of the Lotus Sutra and embody the Law which was trans-ferred to Bodhisattva Jōgyō in the *Jinriki* (twenty-first) chapter for propagation in the Latter Day. The *Juryō* chapter reads, "I will leave this good medicine here. You should take it and not worry that it will not cure you." From the viewpoint of the Daishonin's Bud-dhism, "this good medicine" is the Gohonzon; "I will leave this good medicine here" indicates the place of practice where the Gohonzon is enshrined; and "you should take it" signifies that all people should chant dai-moku to the Gohonzon.

What significance can be attached to the Three Great Secret Laws of Nichiren Daishonin? First, the object of worship was established in the concrete form of the Gohonzon, the embodiment of the ultimate reali-ty of life. The Gohonzon is the basis of the Three Great Secret Laws, for the invocation of Nam-myoho-renge-kyo is directed toward it and the high sanctuary is built to enshrine it. Second, chanting daimoku indicates the importance of one's faith in the Gohonzon and one's practice to it. How much power one can draw from the Gohonzon depends on the strength and depth of one's faith. One's attitude toward faith is a decisive factor in bringing forth the power of the Gohonzon. Thus, the individual is responsible for his own destiny, and his faith is a prerequisite for his happiness. Third, the high sanctuary exists in the realities of society, not somewhere else apart from it. The ideal world one seeks to attain through faith in the Gohonzon is to be found within the realm of daily life. In the practice of faith, the high sanctuary is found precisely where people live, and the place where happiness must be built is the very world in which they conduct their activities.

3. The Gohonzon

RELIGION can work only when its founder's teachings are correctly put into practice. The higher religions expound their views on life and the universe and, on the basis of these views, provide guiding principles for daily living, both personal and social. One's understanding of life and the universe in the framework of a given religion may come under the category of reason. However, the impetus for the practice of any religion lies in the desire to identify with the founder's life and understanding. The actions designed to achieve this generally take on some form of worship.

On the other hand, the forms of worship pursued in the more prominent religions, such as Buddhism, Christianity and Islam, were not stipulated by the founders themselves. Almost all forms of worship have been established later by their disciples. Almost all the founders expressed their ideas about the object of worship in abstract terms, without delineating any concrete form.

Nichiren Daishonin, however, established the object of worship himself, and bequeathed it as the core of faith to all his followers to come. It is called the Gohonzon; the Japanese word *honzon* means object of fundamental respect, and *go* is an honorific prefix.

In the center of the Gohonzon are written the Chinese characters "Nam-myoho-renge-kyo, Nichiren." The Gohonzon is thus a physical object embodying the perfect fusion of the ultimate Law of the universe or Nam-myoho-renge-kyo, and the Person, the original Buddha of *kuon ganjo* or Nichiren Daishonin. To the right and left of these central characters are inscribed the names of those beings which represent each of the Ten Worlds with which one's life is perfectly endowed. The names of Buddhas, bodhisattvas and others are inscribed, as described in the majestic Ceremony in the Air depicted in the Lotus Sutra. The Gohonzon embodies at once the ultimate Law permeating all life and the life of Nichiren Daishonin who has been enlightened to it.

Chanting daimoku with faith in the Gohonzon calls forth from within Nam-myoho-renge-kyo, the Law of life. In this way, one fuses one's life with the Gohonzon. Only through this fusion can one attain the objective of one's practice—Buddhahood. Nichiren Daishonin teaches that "embracing the Gohonzon is in itself enlightenment." This is the principle of attaining Buddhahood in one's present form as a common mortal.

All individual Gohonzon enshrined in the homes of believers or in community centers derive from the Dai-Gohonzon, which Nichiren Daishonin inscribed on October 12, 1279. In other words, they are transcriptions of the Dai-Gohonzon. Wherever one believes in the Gohonzon and chants sincerely, one is able to manifest the Buddha nature and attain Buddhahood. The Dai-Gohonzon was inscribed in Chinese characters by the Daishonin's own hand. That these characters were written by himself on the Dai-Gohonzon has profound significance. They express the inner life of the founder as it was when he inscribed them. The characters themselves thus become an expression of the life of the Daishonin.

4. Nam-myoho-renge-kyo

NAM-MYOHO-RENGE-KYO is the expression of the ultimate truth of life. It also signifies the enlightened life of the Buddha. *Namu* or *nam* derives from the Sanskrit word *namas* and means devotion, or the perfect fusion of one's own life with the eternal truth. Similarly the English word "religion," which derives from Latin, originally meant to bind strongly to something, and so it is also included in the meaning of the word *namu*. Yet the significance of *namu* is twofold. One meaning is, as mentioned above, to dedicate one's life to, or to fuse one's life with, the eternal unchanging truth. The other is that, through this fusion of one's life with the ultimate truth, one simultaneously draws forth infinite energy, as well as inexhaustible wisdom which functions in accordance with the changing circumstances.

What is the eternal truth with which one fuses one's own life? It is Myoho-renge-kyo, which is also the title of the Lotus Sutra as it was translated into Chinese by Kumārajīva. *Myoho* literally means the Mystic Law. *Myo* (mystic) signifies "unfathomable," and *ho* means "law." *Myoho* is the law which exists within the incomprehensible realm of life. However, this is but one interpretation of *myoho*. In another interpretation, *myo* indicates life's true nature or ultimate reality, and *ho* means all phenomena. In terms of the principle of *ichinen sanzen*, *myo* indicates the life that is manifest at each moment (*ichinen*), and *ho*, the three thousand (*sanzen*) varying aspects and phases which it assumes. All things at one time or another assume the aspect of temporary existence which constantly changes, and at other times are in the state of non-substantiality. No matter how the fundamental entity may be manifested, it is itself persistent and eternal. Phenomena (*ho*) are changeable, but pervading all such phenomena is a constant reality. This reality is called *myo*.

Renge means lotus flower. The lotus blooms and produces seeds at the same time, and thus represents the simultaneity of cause and effect, which is one expression of the Mystic Law. Simultaneous cause and effect means essentially that the future can be determined by present causes. Thus the law of cause and effect is also the principle of personal responsibility for one's own destiny. However, because the innermost depths of life are independent of the karma accumulated as the result of past deeds, it is possible to create true happiness, irrespective of karma. This is also represented by another quality of the lotus. It grows and blooms in a muddy pond, and yet is free from any defilement, which symbolizes the emergence of Buddhahood from within the life of a common mortal. In other words, the innermost nature of life remains untainted despite the evil causes that may have been made. *Renge* thus means to reveal the most fundamental nature of the reality of life.

Finally, *kyo* means sutra, the voice or teaching of a Buddha. In a broader sense, it includes the activities of all living beings and of all phenomena in the universe. The Chinese character for *kyo* originally meant a warp of cloth, symbolizing the continuity of life throughout the past, present and future. Moreover, *kyo* indicates that the Buddha's enlightenment, which was embodied as Myoho-renge-kyo, is to be preserved and transmitted for all eternity.

5. The High Sanctuary

THE purpose of keeping Buddhist precepts is "to stem injustice and stop evil" within oneself. The precepts were taught in order to prevent actions against the Buddha's teaching and consequent unhappiness. In the early days after Shakyamuni Buddha's passing, precepts were very highly valued, and Hinayana Buddhism in particular established a great number of them. The basic precepts include the injunctions not to kill, not to steal, and not to tell a lie. As the groups in the Buddhist priesthood increased, the number of precepts also increased. The 250 precepts and the 500 precepts were established as the complete rules of discipline for ordained monks and nuns, respectively. To observe precepts came to be the most important characteristic of Hinayana Buddhism.

Perhaps it was natural that a movement arose against Hinayana in reaction to the increasing number of complicated precepts. This movement was later to be called Mahayana Buddhism, which valued Shakyamuni's spirit above the precepts, and which greatly simplified them. Both Hinayana and Mahayana have *kaidan,* the Japanese word for sanctuary, which means a place in which persons who have decided to live according to the Buddha's teachings vow to observe the precepts and monastic rules. *Kai* literally means precepts, and *dan* indicates an elevated platform established for ordination. Thus, *kaidan* means a sanctuary where vows are taken in a ceremony. In Nichiren Daishonin's Buddhism, there are no precepts other than the one to embrace the Gohonzon and chant Nam-myoho-renge-kyo; therefore, the place where one chants daimoku to the Gohonzon is the high sanctuary.

In 1279 Nichiren Daishonin inscribed the object of worship in fulfillment of the purpose of his advent and entrusted it to all humankind, for both that time and the future. This object of worship is the Dai-Gohonzon which is now enshrined in the Shō-Hondō (Grand Main Temple) in the precincts of Taiseki-ji. The places in which individual Gohonzon, which are transcriptions of the Dai-Gohonzon, are enshrined can also be called sanctuaries. ·

6. Kōsen-rufu

KŌSEN of *kōsen-rufu* literally means to "widely declare," that is, to teach Buddhist philosophy to all people, and *rufu*, "to be spread," means that Buddhism is both well known and sincerely practiced by people in society. Thus *kōsen* indicates the propagation of Buddhism, and *rufu*, the condition which results from this propagation.

The role of ancient religions was to safeguard or secure the prosperity of individual races or tribes. In contrast, the higher religions went beyond races and tribes to seek the universal truth of the human being. Higher religions had the possibility of being widely accepted and were established in order to bring happiness to all humankind.

The Lotus Sutra prophesies that the true teachings of Buddhism will be revealed after the decline of Shakyamuni's Buddhism, and emphasizes that these teachings should be propagated throughout the world. Hearing this declaration, Shakyamuni's disciples and bodhisattvas from other worlds asked Shakyamuni to entrust them with the mission of propagating the true teachings in the future. However, Shakyamuni declined their request, saying that they were not qualified to propagate it because they would not be able to endure the tremendously difficult obstacles that would surely arise in the age to come. It was at just this time that multitudes of bodhisattvas emerged from beneath the earth. They were the bodhisattvas whom Shakyamuni entrusted with the mission of propagating the Law.

In exact accord with the Lotus Sutra's prophecy, just when all of Shakyamuni's teachings and their practices had become inappropriate or had lost the power of saving the people, Nichiren Daishonin established his Buddhism by identifying Nam-myoho-renge-kyo as the Law to be declared and spread widely during the Latter Day of the Law. He embodied his complete enlightenment in the form of the Dai-Gohonzon. This Dai-Gohonzon, he proclaimed, was bestowed upon all human beings for the sake of their peace and happiness. He had already inscribed other Gohonzon which were given to individual believers, but only the Dai-Gohonzon was specifically inscribed, on October 12, 1279, as the object of worship for all people around the world.

Nichiren Daishonin established the Dai-Gohonzon with the conviction that all people would take faith in it. This is called the *kōsen-rufu* of the entity of the Law. The time when many people in the world come to recognize this Dai-Gohonzon as their object of worship is called the *kōsen-rufu* of substantiation, or the widespread acceptance of faith. With the inscription of the Dai-Gohonzon, the entity of the Law, Nichiren Daishonin himself has achieved *kōsen-rufu* in terms of the entity of the Law. The mission of all followers of Nichiren Daishonin is now to attain the *kōsen-rufu* of substantiation by awakening and converting people to the Daishonin's teaching.

7. Person and Law

ACCORDING to Nichiren Daishonin's teaching, the Person and the Law are one. The Person is the original Buddha who made his advent as Nichiren Daishonin, the Buddha of the Latter Day of the Law, and the Law is Nam-myoho-renge-kyo embodied in the Gohonzon, the object of worship for all humankind. The original Buddha is the Buddha of *kuon ganjo* who since the infinite past has been enlightened to the ultimate truth. The Law of Nam-myoho-renge-kyo has also existed since the infinite past and pervades the entire universe while at the same time functioning within one's own life. Because Nichiren Daishonin realized and manifested the eternal Law of Nam-myoho-renge-kyo within himself, he is in this sense the embodiment of Nam-myoho-renge-kyo—the Buddha who is one with the Law. He embodied his enlightened state of life in the form of a mandala called the Gohonzon; thus the Gohonzon also embodies the oneness of Person and Law.

Those who believe in the Gohonzon and pursue their practice with enthusiasm and sincerity are aiming at attaining the ultimate state of oneness of Person and Law. People who are approaching this state but have not yet attained it often become troubled and perplexed as to what to do. Sometimes they stumble. It is a mistake to see only the weaknesses and failures of those who are trying to achieve self-reformation through faith and practice, and to criticize them or claim that Buddhism is invalid. No one can condemn them for not having as yet realized the oneness of Person and Law. Nichiren Daishonin warned against such attitudes in a letter he wrote to Lord Matsuno, saying that believers in the True Law must never slander each other, because all those who embrace and uphold the True Law are Buddhas without exception, and one who slanders a Buddha is committing a grave offense.

In short, the oneness of Person and Law can be attained only by those who practice with faith in the Gohonzon. However, even as people exert themselves, they are in the process of attaining Buddhahood. They are on the way toward attaining Buddhahood, so it is a believer's responsibility to try to make up for other members' weaknesses and to help them. One should base one's practice on the Gohonzon, the entity of the oneness of Person and Law, and follow the teachings of Nichiren Daishonin, who personified the Law of Nammyoho-renge-kyo. In the Gosho, the Daishonin says that one should rely on the Law, not on persons; one must follow the teachings of the Gosho instead of someone's arbitrary words. The fundamental spirit of Nichiren Daishonin's Buddhism has always been to believe in the Gohonzon and put the Gosho, which are his writings, into practice.

8. Master and Disciple

MASTER and disciple are one, and because they are one, although they are independent of each other, there is no essential difference between them. Equality is the most important factor in that specific relationship, but why the emphasis on the oneness of master and disciple? The answer is most simply that in Buddhism the Law is the basis of everything. The mentor means a Buddha, one enlightened to the Law. A disciple is a person who is in the process of becoming enlightened to the Law. They differ, therefore, only in whether or not they are enlightened to the Law. Yet there is an important difference between an enlightened person and an unenlightened one. A mentor expounds the teaching of his enlightenment in order for his disciples to realize the Law, and thereby attempts to make them perfectly equal to him. In the final analysis, therefore, both are equal before the Law, and they are united from the viewpoint of the Law. Herein lies the significance of the oneness of master and disciple.

This view presents a sharp contrast with the Judeo-Christian idea of the distinction between God and human beings, in which God's will and word are regarded as law. When Jesus Christ is regarded as the mentor and his followers as disciples, a rigid distinction is made between the two.

In Nichiren Daishonin's Buddhism the relation between mentor and disciple is based on the principle of perfect equality. The mentor is Nichiren Daishonin and his disciples are those who propagate his teachings. During the Ceremony in the Air expounded in the Lotus Sutra both Nichiren Daishonin and his disciples appeared together, the Daishonin as their leader and his followers as the Bodhisattvas of the Earth.

The Bodhisattvas of the Earth have always existed inherently within the universal life of the Mystic Law.

The life of the Mystic Law is "earth," as described in the Lotus Sutra. Because they emerge from the earth of the Mystic Law, they are called the Bodhisattvas of the Earth. Because they exist in the infinite life of the Mystic Law, they are in the state of Buddhahood. Thus here, too, mentor and disciple are essentially one.

The oneness of master and disciple is a philosophical as well as practical concept. Disciples are able to reach the same state of Buddhahood as their master by practicing the teachings of the latter. In Nichiren Daishonin's Buddhism, this is the direct way to enlightenment, that is, to believe in the Gohonzon and practice according to the Daishonin's teachings. When viewed from the mission of propagation, moreover, mentor and disciple differ in role, so it is a mistake to interpret "oneness" as meaning that disciples must do nothing but learn from their master and follow him. In their own area and field of endeavor, disciples must take over in the commitment to propagate Buddhism. Disciples completely share the responsibility with their mentor. Of course the two do not necessarily have to live together in the same time and place. Their relationship goes beyond the limitations of time and space and is the most ideal type of human relationship.

9. Three Virtues

IN the Gosho known as "The Opening of the Eyes," Nichiren Daishonin identifies himself as the Buddha of the Latter Day of the Law, who possesses the three virtues of sovereign, teacher and parent. At the beginning he states, "There are three categories of people that all men and women should respect. They are the sovereign, the teacher, and the parent."* One must possess the virtues represented by all three in order to be qualified as the Buddha. By respecting Nichiren Daishonin as sovereign, teacher and parent, all people can attain the same state of Buddhahood as Nichiren Daishonin did. The Buddha nature is already inherent in all human lives; only by striving to carry out Buddhist practice, thereby bringing out this Buddha nature from within, can one make it manifest in one's life and attain enlightenment in this lifetime.

The idea of sovereign, teacher and parent does not connote mandatory or compulsory obedience to leaders, teachers or parents. Rather, it represents the virtues that the Buddha possesses. The virtue of sovereign signifies the power to protect the people and to ensure their welfare. The virtue of teacher suggests the power to give the people knowledge and wisdom, and to enable them to act on the basis of correct judgment. The virtue of parent is the power to embrace people with compassion, to protect them from harm and to enable them to develop the ability to live under their own power.

In terms of the three bodies of the Buddha, the virtue of sovereign corresponds to the Dharma body, or the property of the Law, which means that the virtue of sovereign is inherent within life itself. The virtue of teacher corresponds to the bliss body, or the property of wisdom, and the virtue of parent indicates compassion

*Major Writings, vol. 2, p. 71.

and therefore corresponds to the manifested body, or the property of action, which enables the Buddha to carry out compassionate actions to save people.

Since a human being's existence is biological in nature, he can neither be born into the world nor live without protection from his parents. The period required for upbringing is longer for human beings than for any other living creature. Humans are also intellectual beings, and therefore the benefits bestowed by their teachers are indispensable. To be truly human, people require a great deal of knowledge and wisdom. Furthermore, people are social beings, and they depend on the benefits of society. To live a truly satisfying life, humankind requires a more complex and more organized society than other beings.

Thus, these three virtues of sovereign, teacher and parent represent qualities that one should strive to develop, for these are the standards that determine one's true dignity as a human being. The Buddha, however, is fully endowed with and manifests all three virtues for all the beings of this world.

10. Three Treasures

ONE of the most important teachings in Buddhism is the concept of the three treasures: the Buddha, the Law and the Priesthood. These three are called treasures because they are to be revered and valued most highly. The treasure of the Buddha is not a treasure possessed by the Buddha or a treasure respected by the Buddha, but is the Buddha himself. The Buddha indicates one who has become spiritually awakened to the Law of life and the universe, and one who, with immense compassion, leads all people to Buddhahood. This is why the Buddha commands the highest honor and respect.

"Law" means the teachings expounded by the Buddha, which is bequeathed to future generations through his wisdom and power. By practicing this Law, all people can attain Buddhahood. Therefore, the Law is also a treasure of great worth.

"Priesthood" is a group of persons who inherit the Buddha's spirit, preserve the Law and transmit it throughout the world and into the future. No matter how great the Law is, it can never spread of its own accord, so it must be propagated by the people, who practice and teach it. Therefore, the Priesthood is considered the third priceless treasure.

In Shakyamuni's Buddhism, the treasure of the Buddha is Shakyamuni, the treasure of the Law is the Lotus Sutra and the treasure of the Priesthood is Bodhisattvas Fugen and Monju. In the Latter Day of the Law, the three treasures are defined as Nichiren Daishonin (the Buddha), the Dai-Gohonzon bestowed upon all humankind (the Law) and Nikkō Shonin, the Daishonin's immediate successor (the Priesthood).

11. Nichiren Daishonin and Shakyamuni

IN Nichiren Daishonin's Buddhism, Nichiren Daishonin is the true Buddha who revealed his original enlightenment and expounded the ultimate truth in its entirety, and Shakyamuni is a provisional Buddha who assumed a transient role or aspect in order to save the people. The true Buddha and a provisional Buddha may be likened to a substantial body and its reflection, as discussed in the relationship between the theoretical teaching (first half) of the Lotus Sutra and the essential teaching (latter half) of the sutra. The ultimate reality of life realized by all Buddhas, as well as the original cause for their enlightenment, is Nam-myoho-renge-kyo. Therefore, the Buddha who directly reveals and embodies the Law of Nam-myoho-renge-kyo is called the Buddha of *kuon ganjo,* or time without beginning; he is the true Buddha. Viewed in light of the Law of Nam-myoho-renge-kyo, the manifestation of the Buddha of *kuon ganjo* is Nichiren Daishonin. He established the invocation of Nam-myoho-renge-kyo on April 28, 1253, and devoted himself to its propagation. Later, on October 12, 1279, he embodied this Law in the form of the Dai-Gohonzon.

Shakyamuni, on the other hand, taught the Lotus Sutra to explain the Buddha's life, but did not clarify its essence, that is, Nam-myoho-renge-kyo itself. Since Shakyamuni did not reveal Nam-myoho-renge-kyo, he can only be defined as a provisional Buddha who first attained Buddhahood by practicing the ultimate Law countless kalpas ago.

It may appear that Nichiren Daishonin, who is the Buddha from time without beginning, and Shakyamuni, the Buddha who attained enlightenment in *gohyaku-jintengō,* are completely separate. But since Shakyamuni is also a Buddha, the ultimate Law he realized is none other than Nam-myoho-renge-kyo. For this reason he can be thought of as a manifestation of the Buddha of *kuon ganjo* who is eternally enlightened to Nam-myoho-renge-kyo. Shakyamuni appeared in this world, assuming a provisional status, in order to conduct the Ceremony in the Air, depicted in the Lotus Sutra, in which the essence of the sutra was expounded. Bodhisattva Jōgyō and the other Bodhisattvas of the Earth, as well as all other Buddhas present at the ceremony of the Lotus Sutra, may likewise be viewed as manifestations of provisional aspects of Nichiren Daishonin, the Buddha of Nam-myoho-renge-kyo.

12. Three Proofs

NICHIREN Daishonin elucidated three proofs that provide a clear standard for judging the validity of religions. These three are documentary, theoretical and actual proofs. They had already been used extensively long before Nichiren Daishonin's time. They were applied by the various schools of Buddhism that developed after the death of Shakyamuni Buddha to evaluate each other's doctrines.

In Buddhism, documentary proof is used to judge whether or not the ideas held by a particular sect or a

scholar are in agreement with the sutras. After Shakyamuni Buddha's death his disciples recorded all the
teachings that he had expounded during his lifetime.
The sutras are, therefore, regarded as the complete collection of all of his teachings, and because of this, an idea
or interpretation which is not based on them cannot be
considered Buddhist. Nichiren Daishonin bequeathed
many writings to his disciples and lay followers, called
Gosho. These have become the present-day standard to
determine the validity of an argument in a Buddhist
debate. Any idea which is not based on the Gosho or
which contradicts its spirit is not valid in terms of documentary proof.

Theoretical proof, or proof based on sound reasoning, is proof based on an evaluation as to whether or not
the teachings of a religion are compatible with reason.
Reason has its limits, since it must be based on intellectual understanding in order to be valid, but a true religion must be perfectly compatible with reason in any
area which reason can penetrate. A religion cannot be
called true if it contradicts thoroughly verifiable facts
or sound reasoning based on these facts. Theoretical
proof also requires consistency based on common sense,
as well as verifiable scientific findings or theories.

Actual proof is the measure of whether or not the
teachings of a religion are borne out by actual results
when put into practice. Actual proof in religion corresponds to verification through experiments or practical
tests in science, engineering and other technical fields.

When the doctrine, faith and experience of believers
of a religion perfectly measure up to these three proofs,
its validity can be said to be proven. Nichiren Daisho-

nin himself attached the greatest importance to actual proof. He states in the "Three Tripitaka Masters Pray for Rain" that he has found documentary and theoretical proofs to be vital in judging the validity of Buddhist teachings, but that the proof of actual fact surpasses both.* Thus, whether or not a Buddhist sect upholds the correct teachings should be determined not by reputation or power, but according to these three proofs.

13. Five Guides for Propagation

THE five guides (*gokō*) are the criteria Buddhists should take into consideration in propagating faith. They are: (1) a correct understanding of the teaching, (2) a correct understanding of the people's capacity, (3) a correct understanding of the time, (4) a correct understanding of the country, and (5) a correct understanding of the sequence of propagation.

The first prerequisite can be fulfilled by a sincere and thoroughgoing study of the teachings of Nichiren Daishonin. This has a close relation to the other four. The methods of propagating the teachings must vary according to the times and the social circumstances. To what extent is variation to be permitted? What should not change? Correct judgment on these questions is possible only if one fulfills the first prerequisite.

The second prerequisite, a correct understanding of popular sentiment and intellectual inclinations, can be arrived at through a sincere attempt to understand the

*Major Writings, vol. 6, p. 111.

182 PRINCIPLES FOR PRACTICE

individual concerned. Buddhism is propagated in its perfect form through heart-to-heart communication with others. Without understanding or compassion, one cannot spread Buddhism. It is mutual understanding and compassion that form bridges of communication, enabling one to transmit Buddhism to others in the most comprehensible way.

The third criterion, to clearly recognize the current of the times, means to sharpen one's sense of timing. There are occasions when one should teach Buddhism to others and times when one should not. When one is supposed to put full effort into one's work, it would be inappropriate to neglect one's responsibilities in order to discuss Buddhism with someone. One also needs to have a clear and open-minded perception of the times in relation to the propagation of Buddhism. Our current age, when civilization is in the midst of crises that cannot be overcome by anything less than humanity's self-reformation, is the very time when one must work hardest to propagate Nichiren Daishonin's Buddhism, the philosophy of human revolution.

The fourth criterion, an accurate evaluation of a society and its culture, requires a grasp of the manners and customs as well as the traditional patterns of thought and culture of the society in which one is living. Without this understanding, one will not only fail to spread Buddhism correctly, but will suffer repeated rejection or find that Buddhism has been misunderstood.

The fifth criterion is to comprehend the philosophies and systems of thought that have been spread up to the present. This means that one needs to make a close study of the religions and systems of thought that have deeply influenced society. Moreover, one must be aware of the prevailing conceptions and attitudes toward Buddhism. When one has met these five requirements, then for the first time one can confidently begin one's efforts for propagation, without fear of any deviation.

14. Fivefold Comparison

IN the Gosho "The Opening of the Eyes," Nichiren Daishonin established the fivefold comparison as a standard for the comparative evaluation of all systems of thought and religions, especially of all the Buddhist teachings. This principle concerns the "correct understanding of the teaching," one of the five guides for propagation.

The fivefold comparison can be explained as follows:

(1) Buddhism is superior to non-Buddhist teachings. Buddhism attributes the cause of all phenomena, which bring about happiness or unhappiness, to the causal law of life penetrating the three existences of the past, present and future. In contrast, non-Buddhist teachings generally either ascribe it to such external factors as a transcendental being, parents and the environment, or regard all phenomena as the products of pure chance. In other words, non-Buddhist religions tend to encourage one to rely upon others, while Buddhism provides one with the way to reform oneself and elevate one's state of life, establishing true independence.

(2) Mahayana Buddhism is superior to Hinayana Buddhism. Hinayana Buddhism is the teaching for those of the two vehicles, or voice-hearers and cause-awakened ones, who aim only at personal emancipation. Mahayana Buddhism is the teaching for bodhi-sattvas who exercise compassion for other people, as well as seek personal salvation; it is called Mahayana (great vehicle) because it aims to lead people to the shore of enlightenment.

(3) True Mahayana is superior to provisional Maha-yana. True Mahayana refers to the Lotus Sutra, while provisional Mahayana is the pre-Lotus Sutra Mahayana teachings. In the provisional Mahayana teachings, the people of the two vehicles, women and evil persons are excluded from the possibility of attaining enlighten-ment. In contrast, the Lotus Sutra declares that all people possess the Buddha nature inherently, and that they are able to attain Buddhahood immediately by being awakened to it. The Lotus Sutra reveals Shakya-muni's enlightenment itself, and all other Mahayana teachings are simply means to prepare the people to understand the Lotus Sutra.

(4) The essential teaching of the Lotus Sutra is supe-rior to the theoretical teaching. The theoretical teach-ing includes the first fourteen chapters of the sutra, expounded in the form of a sermon by the historical Shakyamuni, who attained enlightenment during his lifetime in India. In contrast, the essential teaching con-sists of the latter fourteen chapters, in the form of a ser-mon delivered by the Shakyamuni who has discarded his transient status and revealed his true identity as the Buddha who attained enlightenment in the remote past

of *gohyaku-jintengō*. Therefore, the Buddha of the essential teaching is called a true Buddha, as opposed to a provisional Buddha of the pre-Lotus Sutra and theoretical teachings who conceals his true identity, assuming a transient role in order to save the people.

(5) The Buddhism of sowing is superior to the Buddhism of the harvest. The Buddhism of the harvest can save those who have already accumulated good causes, that is, who have already received the seed of enlightenment from Shakyamuni in the remote past and nurtured it through Buddhist practice over the course of many lifetimes. The essential teaching of the Lotus Sutra was propagated during Shakyamuni's lifetime and in the Former and Middle Days of the Law for the sake of these people. In contrast, the Buddhism of sowing, Nichiren Daishonin's Buddhism, implants the fundamental seed of Buddhahood, Nam-myoho-renge-kyo, directly into the lives of the people of the Latter Day of the Law, who by definition have never accumulated good fortune through Buddhist practice in the past. Consequently, they can manifest Buddhahood only by receiving the seed of enlightenment, that is, by embracing Nam-myoho-renge-kyo of the Three Great Secret Laws of the Daishonin's Buddhism.

This fivefold system of comparison evaluates various teachings or systems of thought and demonstrates that Nichiren Daishonin's Buddhism is superior to all. There is also, however, the all-encompassing or absolute point of view, which declares that the Daishonin's Buddhism cannot be compared to any other teachings because it encompasses and integrates them all. In this system, other teachings or systems of thought are examined in the light of the ultimate teaching of Buddhism, that is, Nam-myoho-renge-kyo. Thus, based upon the Mystic Law, all laws and teachings can be seen in the proper perspective and can fulfill their intrinsic functions.

15. Faith, Practice and Study

NICHIREN Daishonin teaches that the fundamentals of the Buddhist religion are faith, practice and study. Faith means to believe in the Gohonzon and to have faith that the Gohonzon of Nam-myoho-renge-kyo is identical with one's life. Strong faith is in itself the manifestation of the Buddhahood inherent in one's life. However, this belief must be deepened and strengthened through the practice and study of the Daishonin's teaching.

Practice is divided into two parts—practice for oneself and practice for others. Practice for oneself means to perform gongyo and chant daimoku, and practice for others means to teach other people so that they may realize the greatness of Buddhism and gain the benefit of the Gohonzon. The practice of chanting Nam-myoho-renge-kyo with faith in the Gohonzon brings one's life into perfect fusion with the Gohonzon to become one with the Law of Nam-myoho-renge-kyo. Practice for others includes encouraging others to take faith, and participating in various activities for *kōsen-rufu* and the movement to spread the Mystic Law. By doing this practice, one is carrying out the mission to save others as emissaries of Nichiren Daishonin, the Buddha of the Latter Day of the Law.

It is important to remember that teaching other people about Buddhism will also bring about one's own human revolution. In this sense, practicing for others is also practicing for oneself. Both kinds of practice, therefore, enable one to become enlightened to the ultimate reality of one's life, that is, Nam-myoho-renge-kyo. For example, young scholars, by studying in their own field of specialization each day, can become an expert in their field. Student-artists may finally become recognized for their work. Continual practice is essential if one wishes to become totally awakened to the reality of one's life. Study means to seek to understand Buddhist philosophy, especially the teaching that reveals the power and nature of the Gohonzon. Further, it means to grasp through reason the points of difference and agreement between this teaching and other systems of thought and philosophies. Since people are rational beings, they can deepen and strengthen their belief through a clear understanding of Buddhist philosophy. To teach and explain Buddhism to others, one oneself needs to understand Buddhist principles. Thus, study also involves both the practice for oneself and for others.

Faith is what is most important for the attainment of Buddhahood. Faith gives rise to practice and study, and practice and study in turn serve to deepen one's faith. With a balance of practice and study, faith is deepened. However, it is equally true that the energy springing from faith is the basis for continued practice and study.

16. Attitude toward Gongyo

THE best attitude toward gongyo (literally, "assiduous practice," consisting of chanting Nam-myoho-renge-kyo and reciting the *Hōben* and *Juryō* chapters of the Lotus Sutra) is a natural one. When a problem arises, one should pray for a solution with the same feeling children have when they ask their parents for something. If one has desires, one should pray for their fulfillment in the same way.

In "Reply to Kyōō," Nichiren Daishonin describes the Gohonzon as the perfect embodiment of his own life. This is what is meant by the principle of the oneness of Person and Law. Nichiren Daishonin is the Buddha of the Latter Day of the Law, who saves, protects and leads people in this age. The compassion to help those who are suffering is akin to the love of parents for their children, and the power to protect the people is comparable to the protective function of a sovereign. The wisdom to lead people to happiness is the wisdom of a teacher. These are the three virtues of sovereign, teacher and parent.

That is why the Gohonzon, as the embodiment of the life of Nichiren Daishonin, represents all three to those who practice to it with faith. It is the source of the parental love to save all people, of the wisdom to enable them to live as truly befits human beings, and of the power to overcome severe difficulties and trials. The most important of these three functions is that of the teacher, which provides one with the power and

wisdom to act on one's own. Simply to depend on the
Gohonzon is not enough; to rely solely on the object of
worship is not the correct attitude. It is important that
as a messenger of the Buddha one propagate this Buddhism in society. Since those who do so are messengers
of the Buddha, they can eventually achieve the same
power, wisdom and compassion as the Buddha himself.

It is not feasible to try to find the solution to a problem only by praying to the Gohonzon and doing nothing else. If one offered a freshly caught fish to the
Gohonzon and prayed that it would be transformed
into a broiled one, such a prayer could never be an-
swered. If one wants the fish broiled, one must do
something about it. Then, too, the act of broiling
requires the wisdom to correctly regulate the heat and
season the fish. In every instance one must make all possible efforts to solve whatever problem one has. By
praying to the Gohonzon, one can activate the inexhaustible life force within one and bring out the wisdom to conduct oneself effectively and correctly in each
situation. The role of the Gohonzon lies in enabling
people to realize the wisdom and life force inherent
within them. They can then live independent lives, un-
swayed by the turbulence of society. In conclusion,
gongyo should be performed with the firm resolution
to draw forth the inexhaustible life force and wisdom
from within.

17. Methods of Spreading the Law

THERE are two methods of propagating Buddhism. The first, known as *shakubuku,* can be described as pointing out the errors and correcting the ideas of those whose view of Buddhism is mistaken or prejudiced. The second, called *shōju,* can be defined as encouraging a deeper understanding of the ultimate truth as revealed in Nichiren Daishonin's Buddhism for those whose perception of the truth is only superficial or partial.

In Shakyamuni's day, *shakubuku* was considered the best approach for those people who had distorted ideas about the Lotus Sutra. *Shōju* was used for those who had little or no knowledge of the Lotus Sutra. Nichiren Daishonin embodied the ultimate truth indicated in the Lotus Sutra in concrete form as the Gohonzon of the Three Great Secret Laws. Therefore, *shakubuku* became a way to teach people who had misunderstood the Daishonin's Buddhism, and *shōju* for those who had little or no knowledge of the Daishonin's Buddhism and no particular prejudices against it.

Although these are two distinct methods of propagation, both are usually encompassed in the term *shakubuku.* Strictly speaking, however, there is a definite difference between them. The important thing is to employ the most appropriate method depending on the situation. If one practices *shakubuku* when *shōju* is more appropriate, one will only cause people to misunderstand Buddhism. Using an inappropriate method creates unnecessary friction and delays the progress of *kōsen-rufu*. One ought to endeavor to correct mistaken views about the Gohonzon, but it is unnecessary to try to change a person's views on life and the world even though one may disagree with them. Rather, one should have faith that if the fundamental attitude toward Buddhism changes and people begin to practice it sincerely, they will gradually, of their own accord, change their views for the better.

18. How the Buddha Teaches

THE Buddha uses various means in order to teach people his enlightenment. These means can be broadly divided into four categories, which are called the four ways of teaching (*shishitsudan*). An understanding of these is necessary in carrying out one's own mission to teach and spread Buddhism, and is applicable to education in general. The first of these is propagation according to the desires of the general public—for example, teaching the validity of Buddhism in secular terms related to problems in modern society, explaining to people that it will fulfill their desires, thus arousing their willingness to take faith. The second means is to teach and lead according to an individual's capacity or understanding. This is used in individual guidance. The third way, also used in individual guidance, is to point out a person's mistakes or illusions in order to rectify them. When one becomes able to understand the ultimate truth of Buddhism through the above three means, the fourth type of teaching is appropriate—to reveal the ultimate truth directly.

The first three ways of teaching are all avenues to the fourth. Ultimately, the purpose of propagation is to awaken people to the same truth, or the Law, and to enable them to attain the same state that the Buddha himself realized. One must never forget this purpose. In effect, enabling people to understand and practice Nichiren Daishonin's Buddhism is the only way to solve the problems of humanity, so that all people may overcome their personal sufferings and gain a new, accurate perspective on their own lives and everything else. If this fundamental goal is forgotten, all efforts will be fruitless.

From the standpoint of education, the first way is similar to helping someone broaden his outlook, the second, to revealing what is in his heart while leading him in a positive direction, and the third, to strictly rectifying his errors and misconceptions. Still, all three are but means to an end. The goal of education is to help students attain the same understanding as and even surpass their teacher. The four ways of teaching therefore have great relevance for modern education.

19. Meaning of Slander

ONE's present acts, whether positive or negative, are the causes for one's future happiness or ill fortune. What one does now produces internal changes which later give rise to specific results or effects. Whether one's acts are good or bad can be considered from two points of view: their effects, and the motives behind the acts. Buddhism attaches greater importance to the latter. The story of King Ashoka is often cited as an example of good causes, or motives, created in a past existence. While Shakyamuni Buddha was begging in Rājagriha, the capital of the kingdom of Magadha in India, a boy made a mudpie and offered it to the Buddha, as he had nothing else to offer. Recognizing the sincerity of the boy, the Buddha predicted that he would become the king of a great empire in his next life. Thus the boy was born as King Ashoka. This account emphasizes the importance of the pure spirit of making offering, rather than the value of the gift itself.

In his letter to Lord Matsuno, Nichiren Daishonin enumerated the fourteen causes of evil: (1) arrogance, (2) negligence, (3) arbitrary, egotistical judgment, (4) shallow, self-satisfied understanding, (5) attachment to earthly desires, (6) lack of seeking spirit, (7) not believing, (8) aversion, (9) deluded doubt, (10) vilification, (11) contempt, (12) hatred, (13) jealousy and (14) grudges. These fourteen types of evil refer not so much to specific actions as to one's evil motives or distorted spiritual orientation. The gravest of all forms of evil acts is the slander of the True Law, the act of condemning, deprecating, mocking or rejecting the correct Buddhist teaching or its practitioners out of antagonism or hatred. The negative effect brought on by such an offense is said to be beyond imagination. It is written in the Lotus Sutra that one who commits slander is doomed to fall into the hell of incessant suffering for countless kalpas. This hell is the most horrible of all types of hells. One who kills a parent is said to stay in this hell for no more than twenty kalpas, but one who slanders stays immeasurably longer. The act of slander is that much heavier, that much more onerous.

Some people, according to another interpretation, consider it slanderous to have faith in religions other than Buddhism, but this is not always strictly true. If people believe in another religion without the slightest knowledge of the existence of the Mystic Law, they are not committing slander. However, if a religion is antagonistic toward the Mystic Law, its believers will unknowingly be led into slander. That is why people who profess faith in such a religion are regarded as slanderers of the Mystic Law. On the other hand, if a religion was established without the least awareness of the existence of the Mystic Law, it does not fall within the concept of slander as such. The error of the persons who belong to such a religion is due to ignorance and not to any malicious intention. Here again, the intention or motive is much more important than the act itself.

It is sometimes said that one who disobeys one's seniors is committing slander, but this is not correct. Naturally, one should follow wise advice, but one must not accept misleading guidance. Shakyamuni's admonition, "Rely upon the Law and not upon persons," is one of the most valuable teachings he left for future generations.

20. Lessening One's Karmic Retribution

"LESSENING one's karmic retribution" is one of the benefits gained through one's faith and practice of the Lotus Sutra. It means that one will experience the effects of bad karma from the past to a lesser degree than would normally be true. In "Letter from Sado," Nichiren Daishonin clearly talks about this principle, citing a passage from the *Hatsunaion* Sutra (Sutra of the Great Nirvana) which reads, "It is due to the blessings obtained by protecting the Law that one can diminish in this lifetime his suffering and retribution."* He states that in the past he despised the votaries of the Lotus Sutra and ridiculed the sutra itself. As a result, he was doomed to undergo terrible sufferings which would torment him over many lifetimes, one type of suffering manifesting itself in each existence. However, because he now denounces the enemies of the Lotus Sutra so severely, he lessens in a shorter period of time his negative karmic retribution and causes all sufferings to descend upon him at once. He goes on to explain it by using a metaphor of the repayment of a debt.

In keeping with this example, the principle of "lessening one's karmic retribution" will be illustrated as follows: Good karma which yields happiness is compared to revenue, and evil karma which causes suffering, to expenditure. Good karma is likened to a deposit, and evil karma, to a debt. Of all types of evil karma, the slander of the True Law is the highest expenditure, and this offense is like a great debt. Therefore, to repay

**Major Writings,* vol. 1, p. 40.

one's debts means to undergo sufferings which are equal to the sum of the debt. One can expiate one's heavy karmic retribution by experiencing that much suffering. However, the offense of slandering the True Law is too grave to be completely eradicated during a lifetime. Moreover, to slander the Mystic Law means committing all kinds of evil acts, because the Mystic Law is none other than the Law, or the essence of the Lotus Sutra, perfectly endowed with all the laws of the universe. Consequently, as the "Letter from Sado" states, over an unimaginably long period of time one must undergo each of the sufferings resulting from slanderous acts against the Mystic Law, harassing one in lifetime after lifetime. It is like repaying a pile of debts in long-term installments.

On the other hand, the practice of the Mystic Law provides the way for all people to make and accumulate great good karma and fortune. Only by embracing and propagating this Mystic Law can one repay the debts of one's bad karma, even that of slandering the True Law. In other words, when one undergoes sufferings and hardships because of one's practice of the Mystic Law, one can minimize and even eradicate the vast accumulation of negative effects of the causes which one created not only in this lifetime but throughout the infinite past. Just as one can alleviate the suffering of one's repayment through the great increase of one's income (fortune), one can experience the effects of bad karma to a lesser degree.

21. Demons and Gods

THE positive nature of human beings is such that they strive toward the happiness of other people as well as toward their own self-perfection. Devils or demons can be defined as the negative forces or influences which interfere with this benevolent nature. Generally speaking, the wide variety of factors which hinder the development of human character can be categorized as those arising from within one's own life, in addition to those from outside.

The external factors are natural, social and cultural. Not only natural disasters but such things as traditional thought and customs can at times operate negatively to hinder one's progress toward self-perfection and the welfare of other people. In contrast, the potential destructive nature inherent within life itself, which is regarded as a function of the devil, is none other than the workings of life itself. Some examples are egoism, craving for personal fame and laziness dominated by force of habit. All these are essentially the products of human desire.

In Buddhism the terms "demons" and "gods" indicate the two opposing forces latent within the environment. But external factors can be recognized either as the function of demons or of gods, depending upon how they affect one. External factors are neither demons nor gods per se. Take, for example, a person wandering beneath the blinding glare of the desert sun. For him the sun's intense heat is like a demon which threatens his life. However, the same sun simultaneously fulfills the role of a Buddhist god in its support of all growing things.

Because of their virulence, bacteria or fungi can be interpreted as demons since they can cause disease and even death, but when used appropriately, they can act beneficially as medicine or food, as in the case of penicillin and yeast. The same holds true for the influences exerted by prevailing thought or customs. Fundamentally, how one accepts and utilizes them determines whether their influence is destructive or beneficial. Just as demons are hostile to gods, so are devils opposed to the Buddha, or more accurately, the supreme state of Buddhahood. Human life is inherently endowed with functions to protect and maintain its existence. Manifold desires and instincts are intrinsic to the workings of life. However, they tend to make a person egoistic and eager for immediate profits at the expense of future happiness. As is often said, some people "can't see the forest for the trees." It is an incalculable loss to humankind when individuals become blinded by mere material prosperity and forget to strive for their own growth and for the happiness of others. One's spiritual strength in pursuit of self-perfection and happiness for others can only be inspired and supported by spontaneous will. For this reason, it is natural that the devilish functions innate in life should tend to interfere with one's benevolent aspirations and actions. Demons latent in one's environment have no meaning until they stimulate and call forth the devilish functions from within one's life. Therefore, the most important thing for those who practice Buddhism is to overcome their inherent negative tendencies with the power of faith.

22. Three Calamities

THE *Ninnō* Sutra (Sutra of the Benevolent King) and some of the other sutras warn that the three calamities will inevitably arise whenever society as a whole becomes disrespectful and antagonistic toward the correct teaching. It is noteworthy that all three, high grain prices or inflation (particularly when caused by famine), warfare and pestilence, are brought about by human beings, and they arise together as a direct result of overwhelming antagonism toward the correct teaching. However, they are not always caused only by the slander of the correct teaching. Actually, many other factors can cause the three calamities. If their causes can be pinpointed and dealt with effectively, these calamities can be abated or even eliminated entirely. For example, when a disaster ensues because of injustice in the social structure, the cause is remediable; by rectifying aspects of society where necessary, it is possible to eliminate the problem. In contrast, if the slander of the correct teaching is the cause, no amount of work or effort to improve the social conditions will have any effect. In that case, the social environment is only one factor bringing on the calamity.

The three calamities represent every type of suffering found in human society, and for that reason all people experience them in their daily lives. The offense of slander results in "inflation, warfare and pestilence" in different forms—in social and natural phenomena, politics and medicine, for example. In many cases, people are liable to look only at such superficial factors, totally unaware of their original cause. Since "inflation" goes hand in hand with shortages of vital goods such as food, it represents the disharmonious relationship between human beings and their natural environment. Wars occur because of disharmony among individuals, including all kinds of conflicts, even marital quarrels. "Pestilence" is a disorder which takes place in both the physical and spiritual realms of one's individual life; mental illness can be considered a kind of pestilence.

The sutras say that the basic causes of the three calamities are human desire and greed, in the case of inflation; anger, in the case of warfare; and stupidity, in the case of pestilence. The concept of the three calamities is therefore clearly inseparable from the three poisons inherent in life (fundamental human evils)— greed, anger and stupidity. It is also closely connected with the concept of the three realms of existence, one component principle of *ichinen sanzen*. Pestilences are calamities that occur within the realm of the five components (*go'on seken*), or the realm composed of physical and spiritual elements. Wars take place in the realm of living beings (*shujō seken*). Inflation is a calamity that occurs in the realm of the environment (*kokudo seken*).

At first glance, the three calamities seem to be only a classification of human-caused disasters, but if one probes more deeply, one finds that this concept is far-reaching in revealing the relationship between calamities and human life.

23. Human Revolution

THE basic reason one practices Buddhism is to achieve human revolution. The phrase "human revolution" was used for the first time by Jōsei Toda, the second president of the Soka Gakkai, in reference to the ultimate goal of Buddhist practice. Human revolution means the reformation of one's life and way of living. In the context of "mutual possession of the Ten Worlds" it has become clear that to observe a person's life for a certain period allows one to discover the basic tendency predominating in that individual's mental and physical actions. A reformation of one's life means a change in one's basic life-tendency over a certain period or during one's entire life. One can achieve this reformation by establishing a powerful, independent self that creates value in every situation one faces.

In a broad sense, culture plays an essential role in the attainment of human revolution. That is to say, culture is not merely systems of knowledge and technology concerning the external world. Culture should provide a base for people to gain knowledge and ideas about morals with which to control their desires and impulses. A society's culture shapes the people's intellect, skill and moral character. It leads them to a way of life specific to the culture. In one sense, such enlightenment is a kind of human revolution. If the morals and ways of living in a particular society harmonize with the social situation, the people will not consider such morals constricting. On the contrary, if people are forced to adapt themselves to a rigid standard which does not suit their hopes and needs, they will feel confined and experience suffering.

As mentioned above, religions and cultures in the past helped people realize self-improvement. However, now that society is so very diversified, almost all religions and cultures of the past have become ineffective. The element now necessary for one's human revolution is the establishment of a true self, to enable one to adjust to these endless diversities. One therefore need not perceive oneself as being confined by a certain social or cultural standard.

Religions of the past did not adequately explain the ultimate entity of life. In the Lotus Sutra, Shakyamuni left an important key to this reality. Even so, however, he did not clarify the entity of life. Nichiren Daishonin was the first to declare that entity to be Nam-myoho-renge-kyo. The human revolution urgently needed to change society today will occur when individuals discover the entity of the true self or Nam-myoho-renge-kyo within the depths of their lives. Discovering it will fill them with new life force and wisdom, and enable them to successfully deal with any situation. Ultimately, human revolution is another expression of attaining Buddhahood.

Daisaku Ikeda, the president of the Soka Gakkai International, describes this process of human revolution and its effects, as carried out by Soka Gakkai members, in the novel *The Human Revolution*. Here Mr. Ikeda sums up the dramatic impact of this dynamic yet harmonious revolution as follows: "A great human revolution in just a single individual will help achieve a change in the destiny of a nation and, further, will make possible a change in the destiny of all humankind."

24. Principle of Unity

ITAI dōshin (many in body, one in mind) is the principle of harmony and unity, taught by Nichiren Daishonin. *Itai* means various bodies, and body means a person's individual being as well as the unique set of relationships or interactions he has with the circumstances surrounding him. Human beings have a variety of natural, social and cultural conditions which directly or indirectly affect the development of their character. Accordingly, the natural process of character development tends toward ever greater differentiation. *Itai* is therefore the overwhelming variety of differences occurring among life's entities. *Dōshin* literally means "of the same mind." Yet clearly all people do not have exactly the same thoughts at all times. Rather, it points to the common desire of humankind to realize ideals shared by all. *Dōshin* is the state in which people work together to achieve a common ideal.

Itai dōshin, then, is a principle which enables people to constructively strive to realize any goal, acknowledging that the individuality and differences among people are essential. Such differences in themselves are what makes an impossible dream possible—when everyone shares the highest ideal. Thus, with even a simple principle like *itai dōshin,* Buddhism shows that there is a way to transcend conflict. It provides hope for inexhaustible creativity, as well as the key for all people to join together in the firm conviction that happiness can be found by everyone.

Individuality is formed as a result of many influences in one's surroundings. Each individual has a desire to express his consciousness and make his existence known, and to gain recognition from other people. This desire is so powerful that any forceful suppression of individuality can lead to swift and unexpected reactions in the form of rebellion or oppression. Forcibly grouping people in ways that tend to extinguish their individuality causes factionalism, or "differing minds." Such superficial unity may be temporarily effective, but it never fails to collapse from within.

The principle of unity taught by Nichiren Daishonin teaches one first to respect other people's unique characteristics and differences. Furthermore, it shows one how to unite solidly with unshakable conviction and belief in the universal philosophy which reveals the dignity inherent in all living entities. With such unity, harmony between the individual and the whole is realized for the first time. Moreover, since it is a unity based on the recognition of the inherent dignity of all individuals, it is a bond which grows stronger and more beautiful as time passes.

As individuals fully display their own unique qualities, their organization will also move more dynamically. A watch has many different parts, but when they are put in their right places in relation to each other, the watch will run perfectly. The same is true of the human body, which has many organs. When taken separately, the organs seem to have no relationship to one another. Yet when they form a united whole, the value they possess is even greater than all the wealth in the universe. No matter how firm unity in the organization might be, if the members of the SGI were all "standardized" human beings with exactly the same qualities, it would hardly be able to play an effective role in the realization of world peace. A large variety of talents and abilities is vital to the realization of its goal—*kōsen-rufu*.

Index

207